To
ELSIE
AFFECTIONATELY

CONTENTS

PREFACE 1

CHAPTER

I. THE HEBREW LANGUAGE IN THE JEWISH CURRICULUM 1
    The Traditional Jewish Attitude Toward Hebrew 1
    The Relationship Between a People and Its Language 2
    Hebrew—The Nerve-Center of the Jewish Curriculum . . . 6
    The Present Indifference Toward Hebrew . . . 10
    A Proposed Remedy 12
    Objectives in Teaching Hebrew . . . 13
    A Suggested Methodology and Its Underlying Principles 16

II. METHODS IN TEACHING HEBREW . . . 22
    The Influence of Latin on Language Methodology 22
    The Translation Method Used in Ancient Israel . 23
    The Revolt Against the Translation Method . . 24
    The Underlying Principles of the Newer Methods 24
    The Newer Methods in the Teaching of Hebrew . 27
    The Need of an Objective Evaluation of Method . 28

III. PSYCHOLOGICAL PRINCIPLES UNDERLYING LANGUAGE LEARNING 36
    General Principles of Habit Formation as Applied to Language Learning 36
        Economy 37
        Self-Activity 39

vii

CONTENTS

Specific Practice	40
Correct Start	41
Attentive Practice	43
Integrated Practice	44
Individual Practice	46
Practice Under Pressure	48
Challenging Beginning	49
Purposeful Activity	49
Specific Principles Affecting Language Learning	51
Language, a Speech Experience.	51
Superiority of Auditory Presentations	52
Law of Association or Conditioned Responses	53
Multiple Sense Appeal	55
Multiple Association and Review	56
Associating Symbol and Meaning	57
The Unit of Language Is the Sentence	60
Social Atmosphere	62
Local Atmosphere	62
Dramatization	64

IV. THE PROBLEM OF READING IN THE JEWISH SCHOOL 70

The Nature of the Problem in General and in Jewish Education	70
Reading Objectives in the Primary Grades	72
Physiological Basis of Reading	73
Fallacies of the Phonic Method	75
Proper Reading Approach and Its Underlying Principles	78
Specific Character of the Problem in the Teaching of Hebrew	82
In Summary	85

V.	THE CHOICE AND USE OF TEXT AND READING MATERIAL IN HEBREW	89
	Choice of Vocabulary	89
	Interesting Content	91
	Children's Reading Interests	92
	Content of Hebrew Textbook and Reading Matter.	93
	Learning to Read vs. Reading to Learn	95
	Procedure and Nature of the Reading Program and Character of the Materials.	97
VI.	SPECIFIC SUGGESTIONS FOR THE DEVELOPMENT OF PROPER READING HABITS AND ATTITUDES IN THE PRIMARY GRADES	101
	General Considerations	101
	General Procedure	105
	Specific Devices and Games	108
VII.	READING SITUATIONS AND STIMULI	120
	The School and the Classroom as a Place of Living and Experiencing	120
	Suggestions for Providing and Utilizing Reading Situations in the Classroom	122
VIII.	THE USE OF PHONETICS IN TEACHING READING IN THE PRIMARY GRADES	131
	General Considerations	131
	How Children Learn to Recognize Words	135
	Specific Steps in the Process of Learning to Read.	140
	Devices and Games	143
IX.	VOCABULARY STUDIES AS A BASIS FOR THE READING PROGRAM	148
	The Word List Trend	148
	Word-counts in Hebrew	149
	Studies of Minimum Essentials in Language	151

CONTENTS

The Need of Basic Word Lists in Hebrew   155
Steps in the Reading Program   159
The Associated Talmud Torahs Word List   160
How to Use the Word List in the Classroom   161
The Junior Hebrew Library Word List   164

X. THE TEACHING OF HEBREW GRAMMAR   169
The Need of a Knowledge of Grammar in the
    Study of Hebrew   169
The Problem of Content and Method   170
Content and Method in the Elementary Grades   173
Content and Method in the Advanced Stages.   179

XI. THE TEACHING OF BIBLE IN OUR ELEMENTARY GRADES 184
The Significance of the Bible   184
Difficulties in Teaching Bible   186
A Possible Solution   188
Conclusion.   192

XII. SPECIFIC SUGGESTIONS FOR THE TEACHING OF
    BIBLE   195
Steps in the Bible Lesson   195
    Subject matter   195
    Aim   196
    Method   196
    Materials   197
    Procedure   197

XIII. HOW TO TEACH READING IN THE *Siddur* (MECHANICAL
    READING)   206
General Considerations   206
Specific Steps of Procedure   212
Games and Devices in *Siddur* Reading   213

CONTENTS

XIV.	A Testing Program in Hebrew	219
	The Place of Testing in the Curriculum	219
	Objectivity in Testing	220
	Some Guiding Principles in the Construction of Objective Tests	222
	Available Test-Materials	226
	The Problem of Standardization	229
	Conclusion	232

APPENDIX A — Type Lesson Plan . . . 235

APPENDIX B — Functional Words and Expressions in the Classroom . . . 251

APPENDIX C — Suggested Word list . . 253

APPENDIX D — Samples of Tests for the First Year . 287

INDEX 291

PREFACE

This book was designed to accomplish the following purposes: (1) to serve as a textbook for students in Jewish teachers' training schools, (2) to be employed as a guide by teachers in service and (3) to be used as a reference book by principals and rabbis, who wish to conduct courses in methods of teaching Hebrew in communities where no Jewish teachers' training schools exist. The author feels that there is a need of such materials and he hopes that this book will meet this need.

This volume is not a concoction of arm-chair thinking and study; it is the product of close contact with actual classroom teaching situations over a period of some twenty-five years. In the capacity of teacher, principal and supervisor, the author has had occasion to observe, test and re-test the methods and devices suggested in this book under a variety of teaching conditions. It is his conviction that they are practicable and helpful, and that they are consistent with recent findings and accepted principles in modern psychology and pedagogy.

I feel heavily indebted, in the preparation of this text, to the late Ben Rosen, who as director of the

Associated Talmud Torahs of Philadelphia, stimulated and encouraged me to carry on my studies and investigations in the field of linguistic pedagogy. I am also deeply grateful to my colleagues and friends who read the manuscript and offered constructive criticisms and suggestions. They are: Doctors Samuel Dinin, Jacob S. Golub, Simon Greenberg, Julius H. Greenstone, Leo L. Honor and Mr. Henry R. Goldberg. My sincere thanks are likewise due to Doctor A. E. Millgram, Education Director of the United Synagogue, for his careful reading of the manuscript and for his untiring aid in preparing it for publication, as well as to Doctor Azriel Eizenberg, Director of the Council of Jewish Education of Philadelphia, who read the proof and made some significant and valuable suggestions. Doctor Samuel Pitlik was also helpful in the reading of some of the proof, for which help I am duly grateful.

HOW TO TEACH HEBREW
IN THE
ELEMENTARY GRADES

Chapter 1

THE HEBREW LANGUAGE IN THE JEWISH CURRICULUM

The Traditional Jewish Attitude Toward Hebrew

The study of the Hebrew language and its literature was always focal in the educational efforts of the traditional Jewish school. In fact, the traditional Jewish school was primarily, perhaps exclusively, concerned with the teaching of the Hebrew language and its literature. Similarly, in the modern Jewish weekday school in this country, the major part of the attention, time and resources is devoted to the teaching of Hebrew.

Jewish parents who are at all concerned about the survival of Judaism, of Jewish values and modes of living, have always felt intuitively that a knowledge of Hebrew is essential and that its study is an indispensable element in the scheme of Jewish education. Indeed, our sages very significantly attribute the deliverance of our people from the Egyptian bondage to the fact that they did not give up the use of the Hebrew language.

The Relationship Between a People and Its Language

Such an attitude toward a national language is not mere sentimental clannishness. It springs from a wholesome intuitive conviction and will-to-live, and it is borne out by modern views on linguistic psychology. A language is no longer regarded as merely a means of expression and communication, which may be exchanged as need arises. It is an instrument of thinking and feeling. We think and feel in words, by means of words. Indeed, students of language have come to recognize the fact that racial experience, mental and emotional habits, modes of thought and attitudes of a people are reflected and registered in the words and the idioms of the language. The Hebrew word *Shalom*, for example, with its rich positive and energetic meaning of totality, health, wholesomeness, harmony, success, completeness and abundance of living in a social milieu, has little in common with its equivalents in English or in any other Indo-European language. Similarly, the Hebrew *Ruaḥ* and *Nefesh* do not have the implications of a disembodied soul or spirit, such as are indicated by their equivalents in English. These Hebrew words have dynamic, life-giving and motor-urgent connotations. There is no dichotomy in the Hebrew mind between body and spirit, or soul. There is also a far cry between the Hebrew *Zedakah*, with its implications of social justice, and the English word *charity* which connotes humiliation to the recipient and self-inflation or condescension to the donor; between the richly meaningful *Torah* and *Law*; between *Raḥmanut*, suggesting love, compassion, even motherliness, and *pity* or *mercy*; between *Mitzvah* and *commandment*; and so on.

Indeed, every language, including English, has a stock of words which are charged with the emotional and intellectual experiences of the people employing it. In our own days, for example, the English word *fireside* has come to assume a new connotation as a result of our experience in listening to the fireside chats inaugurated by the late President Franklin D. Roosevelt. The richer and the more intense the historical experiences of the people, the greater the number of such words and the more intensely charged they are. When translated into another language, they become devitalized and anemic.

Such words are not mere linguistic units; they are cultural deposits. But they cannot be transmitted in isolation. They take on their meaning and gain in richness of association and connotation only through an experiential context. The same word will mean one thing to a person with one type of background and experience, and another thing to a person with a different kind of background and experience. In the past, some of these words succeeded in surviving in the vernacular of the people even after the Hebrew language had ceased to be spoken. They were kept alive by the intimate contact of the majority of the people with the Hebrew literary sources and by the persistence of Jewish forms of living and habits of thinking. Under the present circumstances in this country, where the Jewish patterns of life no longer provide a suitable functional context for these words, the contact with the literary sources remains the only avenue of access to these cultural deposits.

Language cannot, therefore, be taken as a sort of currency or medium of exchange. Words in one language cannot be rendered by their equivalents in another language, without losing something vitally and essentially peculiar to the mentality and genius of the people employing it as a means of self-expression. Little wonder, then, that our Rabbis likened the day on which the Bible was translated into Greek to the day on which the Golden Calf was made, "for the Torah does not lend itself to an adequate translation."[1] It is only through the channels of the Hebrew language that the message of the Hebrew prophets, singers and sages flows freely and purely and reaches the heart undiluted and unadulterated.

Through long ages of experiencing and experimentation with life and its problems, the national group

[1] Soph. I, 7

evolves words and idioms as the medium and instrumentality of its feeling, thinking and insights; and the learner acquires the ideas, thoughts, mental habits and attitudes of the group concomitantly with these words and idioms. As his experience and familiarity with the language and its literature increase and grow, he learns not only the simple denotative or sense-meanings of the words, but also their connotative meaning; namely, the metaphors and turns of expression, the whole complex of associations and clusters of allusions with which these words and idioms have been invested in their long history of cultural and literary development. For example, the feelings and images aroused in us by such simple expressions as *Eshet Hayil, Kiddush ha-Shem, Hillul ha-Shem, 'Oneg Shabbat, Male Ta'am, Mesirut Nefesh, Talmid Hakham*, and a host of others, could never be evoked by their equivalents in any other language. Hence, the people rooted in traditional patterns of Jewish life felt the need of retaining them. "It frequently happens that the translator, vainly seeking an equivalent for a Hebrew word or phrase, realizes that translation deals not so much with words as with civilizations."[2] Our pupil who studies the Hebrew language thus becomes integrated into the group, and his identity with it and its traditions is intensified and deepened. He is then, indeed, in the

---

[2] Max L. Margolis, *The Story of Bible Translations*, Jewish Publication Society, 1917, p. 120.

words of Tennyson, "the heir of all the ages" in the life of his people.

A national language may thus be regarded as the "open sesame" to the national genius or the nerve-center which unifies and integrates the national organism in space and in time. It serves as an intellectual and emotional bond among all the members of the group throughout all ages and generations, and throughout all places of dispersion. By the acquisition of the national language, the thoughts and feelings of the young generation are directed into common channels, which have their sources in the age-old traditions and in the bedrock of the national soul.

Hebrew — The Nerve-Center of the Jewish Curriculum

Hebrew, therefore, is not just a subject like history, current events, religion, and so on. All these subjects are important elements in our curriculum. They make for completeness and rounding out of the Jewish educational process. But Hebrew is the nerve-center of the Jewish curriculum. It vitalizes and reinforces all the other subjects. Without it, these subjects are merely so much information, or just memory content, which, in the course of time, gradually fades away and is forgotten, leaving in the mind stray and desultory bits of facts and data. To construct a Jewish curriculum around these subjects, without Hebrew, is largely to build on quicksand. No real educational results in terms of personality changes and modification may be expected from such a Jewish curriculum. Such a curriculum is, at best, a make-shift; at worst, dangerous self-deception. The knowledge of Hebrew is a sine qua non for a full integration into Jewish living and experiencing.

To quote, in this connection, Michael West, one of the most eminent authorities in the field of linguistic pedagogy: " 'Language in education' is not like 'arithmetic in education' or 'history in education'. These are subjects, and defective instruction leaves a gap in the child's education. But defective language teaching causes a disease at the root of the mind itself. It disorganizes the whole psychic system at the root of the mind."[3] Defective linguistic development is known to go hand in hand with stunted intellectual and emotional growth in the case of both individuals and nations.

For a people, therefore, to abandon or neglect the study of its language is to cut itself off from the roots of its intellectual and emotional life, and to suffer, in consequence, spiritual sterility and loss of national identity and character. It is a matter of historical record that those Jewish communities which wandered

·Michael West, *Language in Education*, Longmans, Green, 1932, p. 16 f

away, in their systems of Jewish education, from the original Hebrew sources have failed to survive. "If history has anything to say in the matter, the lesson it affords us is that the disappearance of the Hebrew language was always followed by assimilation with their surroundings, and the disappearance of Judaism. The Hebrew language is not a mere idiom; it is in itself a religious symbol of history, a promise and a hope."[4]

Indeed, Jewish history provides some very clear and distinct examples corroborating Solomon Schechter's statement. Witness, as an illustration, the fate of Alexandrian Jewry in the days of the Maccabees in contrast to the fate of Spanish Jewry in the medieval period. Both these historic communities enjoyed the blessings of economic and political freedom and of unhampered cultural pursuits, but they differed in their attitude toward the Hebrew language. Alexandrian Jewry adopted the Greek version of the Bible as the Torah and the Greek language as their language. They attempted to transfer the "content" of Judaism into the Greek "vessel" and thereby doomed themselves to assimilation and ultimate extinction. They left hardly an impress on the history of Judaism.

The Spanish Jews, on the other hand, never forgot

---

[4] Dr Solomon Schechter, quoted in Norman Bentwich's *Solomon Schechter*, Jewish Publication Society, 1938, p. 291 f.

that the Hebrew language was the most effective, nay, the sole medium for the creativity and self-expression of the Jewish soul. They maintained intimate contact with the people of Spain and were thoroughly conversant with their language and literature. They even wrote some of their philosophical and philological works in the Arabic vernacular, but in the writing of poetry and liturgical compositions they resorted exclusively to the use of Hebrew. Furthermore, they pursued the study of the Hebrew language with such thoroughness and zeal as have not since been surpassed or even equaled. Their contribution to the development of Judaism and of Hebrew literature remains to this day an inexhaustible source of inspiration and guidance.

Yet, from time to time, the assertion is made, implicitly or explicitly, even by some educators and rabbis, that the language is merely a form, a vessel, and that the important thing is, after all, the content. Where the mastery of the form hampers the rapid acquisition of the content, the form should be sacrificed. A tendency to operate with so-called Jewish-content curricula in English is, accordingly, coming into vogue. But this tendency is based on a conception entirely alien to the genius of Jewish tradition; namely, on the dualism of body and spirit, content and form. Judaism recognizes no such dualism, and a non-Hebrew curriculum is a disembodied soul and is out of the pale of a Jewish traditional program of education. Such a curriculum may be tolerated sometimes as a necessary evil, but it must not be confused with a real or legitimate Jewish curriculum, where content and form are intimately and inextricably intertwined.

The Present Indifference Toward Hebrew

In the light of all this it is disheartening to find a growing indifference in this country toward the study of the Hebrew language even among the lamentably small number of Jewish parents who are Jewishly minded enough to send their children to a Jewish school. A very small proportion of the children attending our schools avail themselves of the opportunity to study Hebrew to the extent of being able to read the Bible and our post-biblical literature with intelligence and appreciation. What may account for this regrettable state of affairs?

Two main reasons suggest themselves. On the one hand, the task of studying Hebrew as a new language is arduous and calls for some sacrifices on the part of both pupil and parent. On the other hand, the results in the teaching of Hebrew in this country have not been, admittedly, commensurate with the efforts invested. With all our improvements in methods and techniques we have not succeeded in the major aim of teaching Hebrew, namely, that of equipping our pupils with the ability to read Hebrew with intelligence and appreciation, and of imbuing them with an impelling desire to dip into the vast storehouses of Hebrew literature. Consequently, a feeling of defeatism with reference to the study of Hebrew has grown upon some Jewish parents. This defeatist attitude is frequently rationalized and articulated into the erroneous and dangerous argument that Hebrew is, after all, only a technical or skill-subject, and may be dispensed with, without doing any violence to the basic aims of Jewish education. The study of Hebrew is, thus, destined to be eliminated altogether, or to be relegated to the exclusive province of the rabbi or teacher — a travesty indeed on the traditional aims of Jewish education, where the training of the laity in the knowledge of the Torah was always the center of emphasis.

Yet, the defeatist attitude toward the study of Hebrew is symptomatic, and throws out a challenge to teachers of Hebrew. This attitude must not be ignored or brushed aside by disparaging criticism. In order to combat it effectively it must be attacked at the roots. Nothing succeeds like success. If we could render the process of learning Hebrew more pleasurable and more productive of desirable results and achievements, we might succeed in restoring the traditional positive attitude towards the study of Hebrew. This implies, of course, improvements in method which are based on the capacities and interests of children. It also implies the need of determining the essentials in language learning and of concentrating our effort upon these minimum essentials.

A Proposed Remedy

There are, to be sure, some factors responsible for the failure to accomplish more satisfactory results in the study of Hebrew, factors which are at present beyond the direct control of the Jewish teacher. These are: insufficient time for Hebrew instruction, undue elimination, especially in the primary grades, and a scarcity of adequately prepared teachers. But these factors, too, may be effects rather than causes, and they may be offset or even removed by a more scientific approach in terms of more selective content and improved methodology. More satisfactory results might eventually induce both parents and children to devote more time to the study of Hebrew. The glow of successful achievement would enhance the holding power of our schools and thus reduce elimination. In the long run, a larger proportion of more adequately equipped pupils would reach our Teachers' Training Schools, with the result that more and better trained teachers could be provided for our elementary schools. Such teachers would raise the level of the teaching profession both from the standpoint of social prestige and material compensation.

Thus the direction of the vicious circle would be reversed.

But the reversal in the direction of the vicious circle can be effected only by a careful and rigorous investigation of essentials in the study of Hebrew. Methodology is, of course, important. We must employ the most economic and most efficient methods in teaching. But the problem of *what to teach* is even more significant than that of *how to teach*. Improved methods without regard to the relative merits of the nature of the content may lead us to teach better that which should not be taught at all. Hence, the determination of objectives and of minimum essentials in the light of these objectives is basic and paramount in constructing a course of study in Hebrew.

What are the objectives in the study of Hebrew in this country and what should be the minimum essentials in content to meet these objectives?

Objectives in Teaching Hebrew

There are, in general, four major aspects to the process of language learning, each of which involves a distinct vocabulary and methodological technique. They are: speaking, understanding the spoken words, reading and writing. Mastery in one of these aspects does not imply or insure mastery in any other. Specific training is needed in each case. It is a matter of common observation and experience that many people who employ the spoken Hebrew with ease and glibness have neither the ability nor the desire to read Hebrew. Conversely, many a Hebrew scholar, steeped in hebraic literature, is seriously handicapped in the ability to use the language in simple conversation. In point of fact, traditional hebraic scholarship was entirely divorced, during the past generations, from conversational Hebrew. The study of Hebrew was widespread, but the language was not used in speech.

Time was, some two or three decades ago, when, under the influence of the renaissance of Hebrew speech in Palestine, Jewish educators cherished the dream of building up a Hebrew-speaking environment in this country. The textbooks and the methodology were directed to this end. The classroom activities consisted of a maximum of conversation and a minimum of reading. The textbooks in the elementary grades consisted largely of scrappy and inane selections, drawn from the immediate environment and everyday activities, which served as a pivot around which the classroom conversation turned. The cat, the dog, the squirrel, and so on, were the main heroes of these selections.

The dream of a Hebrew conversational environment in this country proved to be an illusion. The bits of conversational vocabulary picked up in the Hebrew classroom faded out of memory after the pupil left the classroom or the school, for want of environmental opportunities to exercise this ability. The Hebrew subject matter studied and the methodology employed were not calculated to cultivate the desire and the ability to read Hebrew. The result was disillusionment and a sense of defeatism in the ranks of the teachers, as well as a sense of futility and indifference among the parents in regard to the teaching of Hebrew.

Although the conversational approach still persists in some cases by dint of sheer inertia, a shift in emphasis from the conversational to the reading approach is in evidence. The reading aim in the teaching of Hebrew is more or less generally adopted by Jewish educators, although the reading methodology is only half-heartedly and inconsistently pursued.

But before we turn to the problem of methodology, a specific statement of the objectives in the teaching of Hebrew in this country may be appropriate. These objectives are as follows:

1. To build up in our children the sense of being a link in the chain of the hebraic culture and tradition of our people, as well as to foster in them the desire to perpetuate this culture and tradition within the American Jewish environment.

2. To enable our pupils to read and study the Hebrew Bible, liturgical literature, and selections from post-biblical and modern Hebrew literature with intelligence

and appreciation; and to cultivate in them an abiding interest in the reading and study of the Hebrew language and literature.

3. To stimulate and foster an active interest in the efforts to promote the revivial of the Hebrew language in oral and written expression in Palestine and elsewhere.

4. To prepare our children to participate intelligently and sympathetically in the services and in the religious customs of the Home and of the Synagogue.

A Suggested Methodology and Its Underlying Principles

Now what methodology would serve most effectively to achieve these objectives? Such methodology should be based on the following principles:

1. The textbook material and content in the elementary grades should operate with a literary or bookish, rather than a conversational, vocabulary. This vocabulary should be largely composed of such words and idioms as have been found to be most essential, because of their occurrence-frequency, to an intelligent and enjoyable study of the Bible and of such selections from post-biblical Hebrew literature as the children are likely to read in the higher grades. The extent of such a vocabulary is relatively small, as has been proven by numerous studies of basic vocabularies. Reference to these studies will be made in a subsequent chapter.

Words and expressions which are still functioning in Jewish tradition, in national and religious life should also be included.

2. The psychological processes involved in language development and learning must be understood as a basis for formulating techniques and devices.

3. Like every other lesson, the language lesson should be planned and organized around the natural interests of the children, such as story telling, playing games, dramatization, etc. But we must always bear in mind the fact that interests are largely acquired, not born. It is, therefore, the primary responsibility of the teacher to build up and foster interests which lead to the desired learning as an end. In other words, learning activities should not be turned into play activities, but play-tendencies and activities should be utilized for learning purposes.

4. These materials and vocabularies should be graded and arranged in cumulative progressive levels of growth, with constantly lengthening amounts of lesson units. Ample provision should be made for frequent recurrence of vocabulary on the respective levels, in reading situations, preferably in the text itself, or in the practice materials, so that the vocabulary may be learned in a natural way in preparation for each successive level. All other conditions being equal, the more often one sees a word in a reading context the more effectively he learns it.

5. One learns to read by reading. Adequate provision for reading in the text should be made. But this reading should be smooth and uninterrupted by too many and too elaborate drills and explanations. The textbook should not be turned into an exercise book.

6. Incidental vocabularies, or such vocabularies as the pupil may need at some remotely future time but which do not lead directly to the subsequent vocabulary level, should be reduced to a minimum. The child's mind should not be used for cold-storage purposes and should not be cluttered up with "dead weight" which interferes with effective mastery of that which is most essential. Any superficial examination of some of the textbooks now in vogue will yield ample illustrations.

7. Training should be provided progressively for silent independent reading. Materials should be prepared and adapted within the respective vocabulary levels for this purpose. The *Junior Hebrew Library* project, which will be discussed in a subsequent chapter, is a step in this direction.

8. Techniques and devices should be employed such as are designed to place the emphasis on reading with comprehension, rather than on conversation, translation, and paraphrasing. Refer to subsequent chapters for detailed discussions and illustrations.

9. From the very outset, the method of sense-reading, rather than that of deciphering letters and

syllables, should be introduced. Let the child develop the attitude of approaching the Hebrew words as symbols of ideas and meanings, and not as mosaics of arbitrary and meaningless sounds. The experience of several years of practice under varying conditions may be adduced to prove that such a method is both feasible and highly profitable.

Each of these principles will be taken up in turn for elaborate treatment in subsequent chapters. Illustrations and examples will be provided to lend to these discussions clarity and concreteness.

QUESTIONS AND EXERCISES

1. Compare the amount of time given to the teaching of Hebrew in our modern Hebrew schools and *Yeshivahs* with that given to other subjects, such as history and "religion." Can you justify this "disproportionate" distribution of time?

2. What place did the teaching of Hebrew occupy in the traditional Jewish school of the past?

3. What is the proportion, approximately, of Jewish children studying Hebrew in this country? What are the probable causes for this state of affairs? Can these causes be removed?

4. Is the knowledge of Hebrew essential to full and progressive Jewish living? What evidence can we draw

from our own history and experience? What can we learn in this regard from the history of other peoples?

5. How can you justify the retention, in the traditional service, of the Hebrew prayers despite the fact that the majority of the worshippers do not understand the Hebrew language? Would it be advisable to give up Hebrew as the medium of prayer?

6. What is the extent and type of Hebrew knowledge necessary for complete Jewish living?

7. What is meant by the statement "words are cultural deposits"? What words, for example? How do these words take on the "connotative" meanings? Some educators advocate organizing a course of study in Hebrew around these "functional" words. What is your opinion on this?

8. In what respects, does the study of Hebrew differ from the study of other subjects in our curriculum?

9. What are the feasible and desirable objectives in the teaching of Hebrew in this country?

10. What are the underlying principles of an effective methodology in Hebrew by which these objectives might be achieved?

REFERENCES

BARISH, LOUIS — "Is the Hebrew Language Indispensable to Judaism?" *The Reconstructionist*, IX, 10

CHOMSKY, WILLIAM — "The Hebrew Language Is Indispensable to Judaism," *The Reconstructionist*, IX, 12

MORRIS, NATHAN — *The Jewish School*, Eyrie & Spottiswood, London, 1937.
GAMORAN, E. — *Changing Conceptions in Jewish Education*, Macmillan, Part I, Chapters I, III, and IV.
SCHARFSTEIN, ZEVI — החדר, שילה, Chapters VI, IX, XIII–XVI.
WEST, MICHAEL — *Language in Education*, Longmans Green, 1932, Chapters I and II.

CHAPTER II

METHODS IN TEACHING HEBREW

THE INFLUENCE OF LATIN ON LANGUAGE METHODOLOGY

The question of which is *the best method* of teaching a new language has occupied the minds of educators for over three centuries. During the Middle Ages and up to the seventeenth century the study of Latin held sway. Latin was then a more or less living language and a convenient universal vehicle of thought and communication. During the sixteenth and seventeenth centuries the vernacular languages began to come into their own and to claim admittance into the curriculum. However, the study of Latin persisted to dominate the curriculum as an end in itself, that is, as a means of "disciplining the mind." The emphasis in this study shifted then from content, or cultural and literary values, to grammatical forms and structure. Latin began to be studied by a rigid grammar or grammar-translation method which was severely criticized, in turn, by such prominent early educators as Comenius (died in 1670), Montaigne (1533–1592), and Locke (1632–1704). However, this *gerund grinding* translation method, although held in disrepute in progressive educational circles, is still widely in vogue, in more or less modified form, in our schools.

The "Translation" Method Used in Ancient Israel

The use of translation as a means of rendering and interpreting the original Hebrew Scriptures was already in vogue in the early periods of the Second Commonwealth. According to Jewish tradition, selections from the biblical texts were read during the synagogue services, held on the Sabbath and on Monday and Thursday mornings (market days). These biblical selections were read twice in the original Hebrew and once in the Aramaic translation, since Aramaic had then begun to gain currency in Palestine, Syria, and Babylonia, and had gradually displaced Hebrew as the vernacular. But the translation was free and interpretative, and the emphasis was clearly and definitely on content and not on grammatical analysis. In point of fact the verses had to be read as units and were not allowed to be broken up except in the instruction of very young children who are unable to grasp larger units. The practice pursued was apparently that of reading first a verse or several verses constituting an ideational unit. This was followed by an interpretative translation or exposition which was given orally, without looking into the text. The text was then re-read for the purpose of a smoother and more integrated comprehension of the contents. Such a procedure is not at all unsound pedagogically and could be adopted with profit by some of our teachers who still persist in the practice of dissecting biblical or other literary texts and interspersing them thickly with laborious translations, explanations and drills.

The Revolt Against the Translation Method

During the middle of the 19th century a violent reaction against the grammar-translation method manifested itself in Germany, France, and elsewhere. The recognition gained for the study of modern languages in the curriculum contributed largely to this reaction. Various methods, differing little in essentials, but bearing different designations, came into vogue and were promulgated with almost missionary zeal. The most prominent of these methods are: the "natural," the "direct," and "psychological" methods.

The Underlying Principles of the Newer Methods

In all these methods the basic principle is that language is primarily a speech experience. The natural way to learn a new language is the same as that of learning one's mother tongue; namely, by hearing it and using it in oral expression without bothering about grammatical forms and rules. The connection between symbol (word) and concept (meaning) should be direct, without the interposition of the native word as the intermediary. Hence, the teacher is to resort to the use of pictures, objects, mimicry, gesticulation and acting out in order to convey the meaning of the foreign symbols. The vernacular is to be eliminated entirely or is to be reduced to a minimum. Grammar should be studied inductively, incidental to the oral work, and considerable emphasis should be placed on the study of the civilization of the country which is the natural milieu of the new language. The vocabulary and content must, of necessity, be kept, at the beginning, within the framework of simple activities and incidents drawn from everyday life in the classroom, the home and the immediate environment. Only after some degree of familiarity with the spoken word are the pupils to be allowed to see the words in print.

The "psychological" method propounded by Gouin, a Frenchman, and popularized in English by Swan and Betis, contributed to modern language methodology the emphasis on *mental visualization*. In order to secure a lasting connection between the word and its meaning, it is claimed by the advocates of this method, the learner must form a distinct mental image of the thing, idea, or act presented by the word. Direct physical observation may be misleading and distracting, or may leave only a fleeting impression. The object, picture, or gesture observed may evoke irrelevant ideas and associations, and the foreign words may be repeated mechanically without calling forth any of the specific mental images they are intended to symbolize. A mental image formed with the word, on the other hand, is reliable and will be sure to adhere to the word, so that the one will always recall the other.

In order to facilitate the formation of these mental images, the vocabulary was arranged by Gouin and his disciples in series of short sentences denoting events and incidents related in subject and connected by temporal sequence. These series of sentences centering around a general topic such as the home, the school, the community, the farm, etc., were subdivided into short lessons, each dealing with a specific aspect of the general topic. This method was, therefore, often designated as the "series system." The topical relationship and the natural chronological sequence, it was argued, not without justification, aid in the building of mental images and in retaining them in the mind. In support of this theory may be adduced the *Gestalt* principle, according to which the mind grasps whole rather than simple elements in a situation. When these elements can group themselves into a "series" or pattern of ideas they are more easily learned and more lastingly retained.

The Newer Methods in the Teaching of Hebrew

In Jewish education the revolt against the translation method was set in motion by Eliezer Ben Yehudah, the standard bearer of the modern Hebrew revival in Palestine. Soon after his arrival in Palestine, in 1881, Ben Yehudah began to blaze the path, by propaganda and example, for the revival of the Hebrew language in everyday speech. He launched a violent attack on the schools of *Alliance Israelite,* a Franco-Jewish society interested in spreading education among the Jews of Palestine, for their use of French as the language of instruction, thereby introducing a diversity of dialects in Palestine and undermining the unity of the Jewish people. He urged them to employ Hebrew instead of French as the medium of instruction. When offered an opportunity to teach in one of the *Alliance* schools he proceeded to put his ideas into practice. But the knowledge of the Hebrew language by the pupils was, of course, a necessary prerequisite, for it was inconceivable to use the Hebrew language as the tool of instruction without enabling the pupils to master the use of the tool. But how was Hebrew to be taught? If the other subjects are taught in Hebrew, why not the Hebrew language itself? In other words, Hebrew was to be taught without the use of any other language as the intermediary. Thus, without much knowledge of language methodology, Ben Yehudah hit upon the idea of *Ivrit be-Ivrit*. Ben Yehudah had to give up teaching because of ill health. But his views were taken up and championed vigorously and ably by such men as Yehudah Grazovsky, David Yellin, Izhak Epstein and others. Grazovsky's article, entitled *Ha-Shitah ha-Tiv'it be-Hora'at Sefatenu*, published in 1895, in *Ha-Zevi*, a Hebrew magazine published and edited by Ben Yehudah, was the first attempt in Hebrew to bring this method to public attention in the light of theoretical principles. It was subsequently elaborated and presented with an array of techniques and devices by Yellin, Epstein and others, and it came to be accepted in the teaching of Hebrew in European countries, as well as in America. This method, designated *Ha-Shitah ha-Tiv'it* (natural method) or *Ivrit be-Ivrit* (Hebrew rendered or explained by means of simpler Hebrew) became the rallying point for all those interested in Zionism and in the revival of Hebrew as a living language.

The Need of an Objective Evaluation of Method

Now that the question of the renaissance of Hebrew as a spoken tongue is no longer a controversial issue, the question of Hebrew methodology need not any longer be enshrouded in a smoke of partisan polemics.

Furthermore, a new departure in the study of modern foreign language methodology was ushered in, in 1924, by the organization of the *Modern Foreign Language Study*, under the auspices of the American Canadian Committee on Modern Languages, and financed by the Carnegie Corporation. This study was conducted in a spirit of experimental inquiry and painstaking research. Nearly all aspects of language methodology were thoroughly investigated, and some valuable and far-reaching data were made available. An objective evaluation of the problem, free from dialectics and dogmatism, should now be possible.

The *Ivrit be-Ivrit* method has contributed much toward vitalizing Hebrew instruction in our schools. The humdrum translation method, which is still employed in many of our schools, has been long due for an overhauling. The stereotyped "word-matching" exercises, characteristic of this method, are not likely to result in a real appreciation of the Hebrew language and its literature. Only by dint of much practice and of a combination of circumstances, which no longer obtain in our modern Jewish environment in this country, have some of the products of the old *Ḥeder*, where this method was employed, managed to overcome its handicaps.

The *Ivrit be-Ivrit* method, on the other hand, has succeeded, especially during its early pioneering days, when teachers were adequately equipped and imbued with zeal and unreserved faith in its efficacy, in cultivating a love and a "feeling" for the Hebrew language and a facility in its use in oral and written expression. The conversational activities conducted in the classroom, in accord with the principles of this method, are calculated to allow for full bodily expression and to reduce, or even eliminate, the irksomeness of sedentary classroom tasks. This method brings into play the eye-voice-ear-hand connections in the process of language learning, and it enables the pupils to acquire a sense of the use of the language as a vehicle of expression. The language thus learned is envisaged not as a mathematical combination of dictionary words but as a dynamic pattern of human thinking and intercommunication.

More specifically, the techniques employed in this method during the early stages of language learning revolve around objects and activities which can be demonstrated in the classroom either by actual performance or by means of pictorial materials. As the object is shown or the activity performed, the appropriate word or expression is employed. The pupil thus learns to associate, after some drill, the verbal symbols with the object displayed or activity performed.

For example, the lesson may comprise such expressions as the following: זה ילד, זה כסא, הילד קם, הילד הולך אל הכסא, הילד יושב על הכסא, הילד קורא בספר.

In each instance the teacher points to the object or act and employs simultaneously the related Hebrew expression. She may call on one or more of the pupils to repeat, after her, the particular expression presented. She may also have the pupils, in turn, execute certain commands, such as לך (לכי) אל הלוח, כתוב (כתבי) על הלוח, פתח (פתחי) את הדלת etc. . These commands may be given first by the teacher, then, in turn, by the pupils.

Some of the principles underlying the *Ivrit be-Ivrit* method are sound, and many of the devices suggested by its proponents are helpful and profitable. These devices will be presented in the subsequent chapter. However, many of their fundamental assumptions have not been substantiated by experimentation, while others are entirely untenable in the light of modern research. For example, there is no reason to assume that a direct connection may be established between symbol and meaning at the initial stages of language learning, as maintained by the "direct" methodists. Our thoughts and words are so intimately knit together as to preclude the possibility of displacing the native word by a foreign equivalent, in the case of a beginner, and of making him think in the new language. Willy-nilly the native equivalent will interpose itself and resist the "foreign intruder" despite all the Direct Method devices. Experiments by

Schlüter[1] prove that in 70% of the cases the native word suggested itself in the Direct Method procedure.

In the light of all this, it would seem that in listening or in reading we do not hear the jumble of sounds or see the component letters, but rather an ordered interpretation that we put on these sounds or letters. The meaning is the thing that impresses, the vehicle is lost sight of. Only by a long process of habituation and drill may a direct association between symbol and meaning be built up. Hence, it is perfectly legitimate and sound to suggest the equivalents in the vernacular outright and then to "eliminate" them by means of practice in the context of the new language. The intermediate link of the vernacular gradually fades out of consciousness in the same manner as stations disappear when trains go right on through, and a direct connection is established between the concept and the foreign symbol.

Furthermore, the *Ivrit be-Ivrit* approach must operate in the primary grades, as is clearly evident, with a vocabulary which can be illustrated by means of objects or performances in the classroom. It is entirely inadequate in the case of abstract words, or words which cannot be illustrated by actual or pictorial representations. Such words as היה, שמר, אהב, etc., how-

---

[1] Quoted by H. R. Huse, *Psychology of Foreign Language Study*, Chapel Hill, University of North Carolina, 1931, p 32.

ever significant they may be for reading purposes, cannot be presented in this method, except by indirect circumlocutions and by uneconomical, circuitous devices.

It is also a fact substantiated by observation and experience that the speaking ability in a language takes longer to achieve and disappears faster than the reading ability. Any immigrant, under the age of twenty, who has no opportunity to use his native tongue, will testify to this. After a few years he will lose the ability to converse in his native language, but his reading knowledge, if he had any, will persist long beyond that period.

In brief, to search for the "best method" in teaching a new language is to pursue a will-o'-the-wisp. There is no one method that may be regarded as a panacea, which will serve all purposes and satisfy all conditions. No single method should be turned into a sacrosanct or inviolate fetish. It is not *a good method* but rather *good method* that the teacher should aim to achieve.

But good method in teaching a language is fundamentally the same as in teaching in general. It must be based on sound pedagogic principles, namely: (1) the setting up of clear and definite objectives; (2) the adoption of a procedure calculated to meet these objectives most economically and efficiently, bearing in mind the laws of linguistic development and growth;

and (3) the arrangement of situations which make for clear, vivid and intense stimulation, as well as for wholehearted and purposeful response. Such situations must, of course, be designed in terms of the children's capacities and natural interests, such as physical activity, mental curiosity, dramatic and play interests, and the like.

In the subsequent chapter an attempt will be made to present, as objectively as possible, the criteria of linguistic methodology in terms of specific aims, and of the nature of linguistic growth and development. These criteria may serve as a guide in evaluating our methods and procedures in the teaching of Hebrew.

QUESTIONS AND EXERCISES

1. Describe briefly the various methods of teaching foreign languages. What are the underlying principles of each?

2. What is the origin of the translation method? What are its advantages and weaknesses? How do the newer methods attempt to improve the methodology of foreign language instruction?

3. What was the nature of the translation method among the ancient Hebrews? How did it differ from the translation method employed in the teaching of foreign languages?

4. What is meant specifically by the Direct Method? Why is it so designated? What are its advantages and weaknesses? By what term is this method designated in Hebrew methodology?

5. How did the *Ivrit be-Ivrit* method originate and evolve in the teaching of Hebrew?

6. What are some of the pedagogic principles that good method in the teaching of Hebrew should incorporate?

REFERENCES

BAHLSEN, L. — *The Teaching of Modern Languages*, Ginn, Chapter V.

CHOMSKY, WILLIAM — "Aims and Methods of Teaching Hebrew", *Jewish Education*, XV, 3.

COLE, ROBERT D. — (Revised by THARP, JAMES B.) — *Modern Foreign Languages and Their Teaching*, Appleton-Century Co., 1937, Chapter III.

COLEMAN, A. — *Experiments and Studies in Modern Language Teaching*, University of Chicago Press, pp. 1-99.

GOUIN, FRANCOIS — *The Art of Teaching and Studying Languages* (Translated by SWAN AND BETIS), Longmans, Green, 1915.

HANDSCHIN, CHARLES H. — *Modern Language Teaching*, World Book Co., 1940, Chapter III.

HUSE, H. R. — Reading and Speaking Foreign Languages, Chapel Hill, 1945, Chapter V.

KITTSON, E. G. — *Theory and Practice of Language Teaching*, Oxford University Press, 1918, Part II, Chapters II, III, and IV.

KRAUSE, CARL A. — *The Direct Method in Modern Languages*, Scribner's, Chapters II, VII, and VIII.

MORRISON, HENRY C. — *The Practice of Teaching in the Secondary School*, University of Chicago Press, 1931, Chapter XXIV.

SCHARFSTEIN, ZEVI — דרכי למוד לשוננו, 1940, Chapters I-V.

WEST, MICHAEL — *Language in Education*, Longmans, Green, Chapters III and VII.

Chapter III

PSYCHOLOGICAL PRINCIPLES UNDERLYING LANGUAGE LEARNING

General Principles of Habit Formation as Applied to Language Learning

Human language goes back ultimately, both in the life of the individual and of the race, to stray babbling, reflex vocalization, and haphazard attempts at self-expression and communication. After much experiencing and experimentation, the undifferentiated conglomerates of sounds evolve into words, expressions and idioms, whose meaning grows, deepens and expands with the experience and progress of the individual or of the race.

Learning a language, whether native or new, is therefore basically a process of habit formation. Every language has its own peculiar thought-processes and set of habits: peculiarities and habits of intonation, of vocabulary, of word-order, of grammatical inflections, of syntax, of idiom and turns of expression — all of which constitute the genius of the particular language. We acquire these linguistic habits much in the same manner as we acquire habits of walking, eating, swimming, of conduct, courtesy, and the like. The truth of this is particularly manifest when one tries to understand, speak or write a new language. Regardless of how well the new language is mastered, the shift from one language, especially the native language, to the other, will often entail serious difficulties at the outset: "What is the meaning of this word?" "How do you express this idea?" "How do you translate this expression?" and so on. Only after getting into the "swing" of the new language, the new thought-process and linguistic habits begin to predominate, and the new words and expressions then come, as it were, of their own accord.

A full and detailed statement of the principles underlying the process of habituation would be beyond the province of this discussion. At this point a summary of these principles and reference to their bearing on the problem under discussion may prove helpful.

1. *Economy* — In learning a new habit, it is advisable to devote as much of the available time as possible to the practice of the new habit, while accessory and incidental processes should be reduced to a minimum. It is certainly inefficient and uneconomical to practice a new habit while persisting in the old habit of doing a particular thing; as, for example, in trying to acquire a new stroke in swimming while practicing the old one at the same time. Hence, the advocates of the Direct Method justly claim that repeated trans-

lation from and into the new language is to be avoided, because it is tantamount to attempting to play the same tune on two different instruments simultaneously. The practice in the old language-habits will certainly interfere with the effective acquisition of the mental habits involved in the new language. Besides, the time spent in the use of the old language, while translating, could more profitably be employed in the use of the new language. Furthermore, repeated practice in translating frequently degenerates into an exercise in word matching with almost total absence of mental imagery. It is not at all unusual to find pupils trained by the translation method capable of rendering a perfect translation of a paragraph or a group of sentences in the new language without having a mental picture of what it is all about. When asked to give the general contents of what they have read, they are completely stumped. These pupils have not learned to understand the new language; they have merely learned to match by rote the words in this language with the equivalents in the native language.

However, the procedure, in the orthodox Direct Method, of resorting to long circuitous explanations and illustrations in order to render simple words in the new language without the use of the native language, is also in violation of the principle of economy. Such words are generally translated by the pupils to themselves anyway, silently or aloud. It is therefore much more economical, as was suggested above, to banish the intrusion of the native elements through the following process. Suggest them in the presentation of the "foreign" words, but make them disappear gradually in the practice and drill activities, during which the native symbols should as far as possible be barred from consciousness.

2. *Self-activity* — The old conception of teaching as a process of "pouring in" and of learning as a process of "absorbing" has been thrown into discard. Learning, in the modern sense, is an active process and is based on pupil experience and activity: motor, intellectual, or emotional. The function of the teacher is merely to stimulate, guide, and direct this process. To learn means to acquire new and definite responses by reacting adequately. When an animal learns to perform certain tricks in response to certain words, commands, or gestures, it does not absorb into its "consciousness" the form or image of these words or gestures; it cannot repeat or reproduce them; it has merely learned to react to them.

In learning the meaning of the printed or auditory symbol אָכַל, for example, we may have but a vague and an indistinct visual or auditory image of the word, and we may, therefore, misspell it. Furthermore, the meaning of the word is not inherent in its form. This particular combination of sounds or letters may as well mean anything instead of "he ate." But we acquire by dint of practice a certain ideational reaction to its picture which emerges simultaneously and automatically. Hence the learner must be roused to activity and made to react. The *drive* or *dynamo* is in the learner. It is not the teacher or the subject matter that educates, but the responses that the pupil makes to the subject matter presented. The effectiveness of learning, therefore, depends on the extent to which the learner himself is active. It is the teacher's task to create opportunities for, to stimulate and to direct, such activities as will lead to the desired learning. Do not, therefore, allow your pupils to become mere passive listeners. Keep them "on their toes." Always ask yourself the question: "What proportion of the time and of the classroom activity is carried on by the pupils themselves?" Only to the degree to which the children like to respond and are given the opportunity to do so is any language method effective. Refer frequently to the outline of suggestions for activities and games, chapters VI–VIII.

3. *Specific Practice* — As a corollary of the preceding statement, it is clear that we learn only that to which we react. In reading a newspaper or a book, or in listening to a lecture, we learn only those facts and ideas to which we respond. The rest may also be seen, or heard; every word and expression may be clearly comprehended. But we do not form any ideational reaction to it. Hence we fail to learn it. In

like manner we acquire proficiency in translating by practicing translation, in conversing and paraphrasing in Hebrew by practicing the particular ability or skill. Excessive practice in mechanical reading and phonic drills, or in isolated word-studies leads to "deciphering," i. e., to the ability of putting together a mosaic of meaningless sounds, syllables and words. None of these practices leads to the chief objective in the teaching of Hebrew, namely, the ability to "read" Hebrew, that is, to extract meaning from the printed or written material, without focusing attention on the sounds or the words.[1] This can be achieved only through abundant experience in reading thought content. Similarly, learning to spell orally does not make for improvement in written spelling. Nor does the study of paradigms result in correct usage and in the development of grammatical sense. In short, learning and practice should be conducted in the manner in which the acquired learning product is to be used in actual life situations. The fundamental objective should be kept in the foreground of the teacher's consciousness to the exclusion of cross purposes and irrelevant activities.

4. *Correct Start* — "First impressions last longest," provided the impressions are clear and vivid. This popular saying is borne out by common observation and experimental proof. Close attention, vivid curios-

[1] See below, Chapter IV.

ity, and keen interest generally actuate our first learning experiences. Hence the powerful influence of our early responses in a given situation upon all subsequent responses. These early responses are deeply stamped in and are hard to eradicate. Prevention is always the best cure. Attention must be given during the intial stages to the detection and elimination of inaccurate and inappropriate responses. The greater the degree of learning at the outset, the less susceptible it will be to interference and forgetting.[2]

It is, therefore, essential to secure from the very outset a sufficient number of *correct repetitions* and to keep the mind of the learner off erroneous responses and false associations during the early stages of learning. Since initial learning is largely a "hit or miss" process, the teacher should provide for adequate practice of the "hits" and should carefully avoid occasions for "missing." Impressions and explanations should be clear and definite. Opportunities for random guesswork should, as far as possible, be eliminated. When a pupil misses a word in Hebrew or in reading, he should not be asked to "think" it out. "Thinking" is ineffectual where automatic responses are involved. He should be given a helpful hint. Familiar context may be recalled. Where this cannot be done, or where it proves unsuccessful, no time should be wasted on useless

---

[2] See A. I. Gates, etc., *Educational Psychology*, Macmillan, 1940, p. 413.

guessing or thinking which leads to the formation of incorrect responses. The correct response should be given by the teacher or, preferably, by one of the pupils, and it should be put down for special study. Directions to pupils should be specific. Children should not be allowed to read or write the new linguistic material until they have heard and repeated it, individually and in concert, several times. Proper habits of pronunciation, enunciation, reading and writing should be insisted on from the very beginning, bearing in mind, of course, that habits are acquired gradually and by painstaking efforts.

5. *Attentive Practice* — In the process of habit formation, wisely regulated and persistent practice is essential. There is no makeshift for it. But attention must be kept alert. Learning a new language involves considerable repetition and drill work, so that the association between the symbol and meaning may be kept alive. But repetition tends inevitably to become perfunctory and monotonous, and the curious mind of the normal child is eager for change and abhors monotony. Listless repetition is worse than no repetition at all, for it breeds carelessness and distracted mental habits. Hence, many and varied situations must be provided, which will focus the attention of the learner on the linguistic habit to be learned. An appeal to the natural interests of children, such as play and physical activities, can always be counted on to secure earnest and

sustained effort. Pupils should be guided to recognize the mastery of the particular skill as a necessary step to a desired end or goal. This goal may be the execution of some project or festival program, playing a game, dramatizing the selection read, finding out "what's coming next" in the story, a higher mark in the group or individual progress chart, etc. The teacher should have recourse to a large variety of games and devices, such as will make the drill absorbingly interesting and will not allow it to degenerate into monotonous boredom. Frequent reference should be made to the list of games in chapters VI–VIII.

6. *Integrated Practice* — Desultory practice or practice of isolated elements is ineffective. Only insofar as the several elements studied can be interrelated and bound together in a unitary whole, does the practice result in effective learning. Disjointed facts as well as unrelated lists of words and sentences are hard to learn and are easily forgotten. They must be held together by a texture of meaning, and this contextual relationship should always be kept in the foreground of consciousness during practice. When the individual elements A, B, C, etc., are integrated into a unitary pattern in the presentation, they are endowed by virtue of this integration with chemical valence, as it were, or with "membership character," with the result that they are more readily perceived and apprehended and more permanently retained. Whenever one of the

"members" of the total configuration reappears, its "membership character" will manifest itself by evoking the other "members" of the configuration and by tending to supplement itself with them.

For example, in learning the sentence בראשית ברא אלהים את השמים ואת הארץ each of the component words is much more clearly comprehended and much more lastingly remembered by virtue of its association with the rest of the words in the sentence. The word ברא, for instance, will suggest the rest of the sentence, whereby the meaning of this word is brought clearly into relief. Similarly, the context of the creation story lends clarity, coloring and retentiveness to the sentence. Words, as well as sentences, studied in isolation are loose and deciduous; they leave but a fleeting and vague impression on the mind. Occasionally, the parts must be singled out for specific treatment and reinforcement by practice, but only after their respective position in the total pattern has been more or less definitely established. A framework of coherence for words and sentences is essential as a basis for effective language learning. This framework may be in the form of a story, a "series," a topic, a project, and the like.

It is, accordingly, a misuse of drill to concentrate attention on certain steps of a process apart from the meaning of the process as a whole. Practice in phonetics, in vocabulary study, in the study of grammatical rules, in spelling, etc., must follow upon an understanding of the larger meaning of the whole to which these items belong. Such practice must also be followed by a realization of how these items function and have meaning and value in the total pattern in which they belong and fit, namely in actual lifelike situations.

7. *Individual Practice* — The fact that children vary considerably in their capacities, in their readiness to respond and in their rate of progress is now taken for granted. No language method can afford to ignore this fact. However, intelligence is generalized rather than specialized. Investigations fail to reveal any such special aptitude as that for learning a new language. The range of intelligence is comprehensive and includes a variety of abilities. Any child who does well in his general school work, all other conditions being equal, is likely to do well in his Hebrew studies. Yet, it must be conceded that children differ in their reactions. Although they possess an adequate stock of common interests to make simultaneous group work highly desirable, even essential, for language learning; the language teacher must provide abundant opportunities for individualized practice. Some children need more drill or guidance than others. Superior children are found to develop slovenly habits of work and concentration, because the group work does not challenge any mental exertion on their part. Other children may

be intensely interested in the drill, yet feel unhappy because they can make no real showing when competing with pupils superior to them in ability. This should be guarded against.

Whenever possible the class should be divided into more or less homogenous groups, the rapid, the medium and the slow. This will challenge and encourage all pupils to put forth their best efforts in competing with members of their own group, who are of nearly equal ability. If this cannot be done, an effort should be made to distribute questions and exercises judiciously, assigning the more difficult tasks to the brighter and the easier tasks to the slower children, so that each child may achieve the joy of attaining something within the limits of his ability. A highly commendable device is to train pupils to compete with their own records of achievement. The fact that a pupil makes fewer errors this time than he made during the preceding practice period will serve as a sufficient source of satisfaction and as a spur to future growth.

The practice and review materials accompanying some of the modern textbooks, in the form of work books or activity books, are further examples of the efforts to meet this problem. As often as possible, a part of the class period should be set aside for these exercises. The brighter pupils may be assigned extra work, or may be employed as leaders to supervise the work of the slower pupils under the teacher's guidance. (For further suggestions see below, chapter VI.)

In the light of this principle, a method of individual instruction in the teaching of Hebrew, adapted from the Dalton and Winnetka systems, was worked out under the auspices of the Bureau of Jewish Education in Chicago. This method, by which students were allowed to progress individually at their own pace, enjoyed wide currency for a while in some of our schools, and its texts, entitled *Hamitlamed Series*, were used extensively. However, its popularity has since waned considerably. Language is essentially a social experience, and no language method can be effective without making adequate use of sources of social stimulation. Yet this method can be employed to advantage in the case of older or retarded pupils, or in classes where wide heterogeneity in age and in capacity of pupils exists.[3]

8. *Practice Under Pressure* — Considerable difference in progress between one class and another may be attributed merely to the difference in "tempo" in the work of the teachers of these two classes. Both teachers may be equally equipped, and the two classes may be parallel in background and intelligence. But the slow and leisurely "tempo" of the one teacher will engender a sluggish and listless attitude in her pupils and will

---

[3] See Nudelman, E. A. — "Three years of Individual Instruction in the Teaching of Hebrew," *Jewish Education* I, 3.

seriously retard the progress of the class, while the lively and alert practice of the other teacher will spur the class to action and will greatly accelerate its progress. After the initial steps in mastering the elements have been made, and a reasonable degree of accuracy has been secured, some drive or incentive should, accordingly, be used to stimulate practice at a high rate of speed and effort. Questioning and answering should be swift and snappy, without sacrificing accuracy. Slow pupils should be passed by for the present. They can be attended to later, individually or in small groups. Pupils who miss words, for example, in their reading exercises should be asked to note these words or to write them down and to study them during a special period set aside for this purpose. Such periods of practice must, however, be brief, or they may result in overstimulation and nerve-racking. (For suggested games devised on this principle see Chapter VI.)

9. *Challenging Beginning* — In order to arouse a favorable mental set or emotional attitude toward the drill, it is advisable to begin with the easier and more interesting elements. But the beginning should not be made too easy, for the class may start on too low a level of effort. It should be difficult enough to be challenging.

10. *Purposeful Activity* — The process of arousing a purpose is regarded in modern pedagogy as the first phase of a teacher's work. Children have natural

desires and interests to which the teacher can appeal. They are eager to play games, to sing songs, to engage in handwork (coloring, pasting, etc.), to collect pictures bearing on the lessons, to organize vocabulary in the form of a dictionary, to dramatize, and so on. The craving of children for a real story is universally known. They never tire of listening to what happens to their hero, to what he says, what he does, or what is done to him. They will act out his part, or the parts of those about him, as often as they are given a chance, provided the situations can be made real and vivid to them. Here is a mine of possibilities, which the resourceful teacher can and should exploit and turn to tremendous educational advantage. Arouse a purpose in your children to listen to the story, to play a game, to dramatize a situation, etc.; *but have these purposes so organized as to lead the pupils through a series of difficult learning and drill situations, which they must master in order to achieve these purposes.* Use these purposes as incentives and means of vitalizing the drill and practice. It cannot be stressed too frequently that this is not to be interpreted to mean that learning tasks should be turned into play activities, but rather that play interests should be directed to learning purposes and ends.

Specific Principles Affecting Language Learning

1. *Language, a Speech Experience* — Language (*Sprache*, לשון, שפה) as indicated by its etymology is basically a speech experience. Our reactions to it from early life are speech reactions (auditory and motor). Spoken language preceded written language in the history of the development of the race as well as of the individual, and should serve as the basis for learning reading and writing. Verbalization, the act of pronunciation and articulation, is recognized as an important factor in vitalizing thought and stamping in impressions. "There may be all kinds of interrelations between visually apprehended words and words apprehended through their sounds. A further important fact, also quite in accord with all the teachings of modern behavioristic psychology, is that meanings are related to articulations quite as much as to sounds. The pronunciation of a familiar word carries with it in many cases a vividness of feeling and interpretation that no hearing or seeing of a word can duplicate. Vocal expression is, therefore, a matter which the primary teacher must understand if methods of teaching are to be as effective as possible."[4] It is a matter of common experience that verbalized impres-

[4] Charles H. Judd and Guy Thomas Buswell, *Silent Reading*, University of Chicago, p. 150.

sions or acts are more lastingly retained and more easily repeated than those which are not verbalized. The writing of the alphabet in the correct order of succession, for example, is aided to a considerable degree by the verbal association of the names of the successive letters *a, b, c*, etc. This is especially true in the teaching of a foreign language where the auditory impressions are very weak and where no opportunity should be neglected to strengthen the association between symbol and meaning. There is fairly unanimous agreement among authorities in the field that a certain amount of oral work in learning a new language facilitates the reading process to a considerable extent.[5] This has been substantiated recently by the results achieved in the Army Specialized Training Program.

2. *Superiority of Auditory Presentations* — Auditory presentations are clearly superior to any other. Reading and writing require a fine degree of motor coordination for which the young child is entirely unequipped and unsuited. They should, therefore, be reduced to a minimum and to the simplest form of procedure in the early stages of learning. Psychologists universally agree that young children learn new vocabulary better when presented to the ear than when presented to the eye. The facial expression, gestures, intonation, and illustrative action

[5] See Robert C. Cole-James B. Tharp, *Modern Foreign Languages and Their Teaching*, D. Appleton Co., 1937, p. 163 f.

accompanying auditory presentation lend vividness, reality, and intensity to impression, which the printed word can never carry to the inexperienced reader. Only after they have acquired proper habits and mastery of reading do they learn better by means of reading.[6] "Since every one learns oral language before written language and since, in racial development as well, the same order of procedure of the oral phase is true, the speech-motor centers and the auditory centers have a physically far better established organization than the writing and reading centers, which are of comparatively recent development."[7]

The teacher should, therefore, provide a goodly portion of auditory presentations, particularly during the early stages of language learning. The children should be allowed to steep themselves adequately in the sounds of the Hebrew words before calling on them to use these words. (See Type Lesson Plan, Appendix A.)

3. *Law of Association or Conditioned Responses* — When two stimuli, one of which elicits a definite response, are presented simultaneously, after several repetitions, this response will attach itself also to the second stimulus even when presented singly. The response is transferred from the stimulus with which it is naturally associated to the other stimulus not naturally

---

[6] Cf. A. I. Gates, *Psychology for Students in Education*, Macmillan, Revised edition, 1930, p. 339.
[7] Lukens, Herman, *Teachers Preliminary Report on Learning Language*, Pedagogical Seminary, 1896, pp. 424 ff.

associated with it. This is a fundamental law in modern psychology, although it is variously explained by the different schools in the field. Thus the sight of food or the clanking of dishes, or the sound of the word "dinner," makes one's mouth water when he is hungry. Similarly, when an object (or its picture), or an idea (by illustration or acting out) is presented to the learner together with the auditory or written symbol (the word or group of words), the ideational response, that is, the awareness of the object or act, will attach itself as readily to the symbols as to the meanings or concepts represented by them. The words ספר, הילד, הולך will elicit the same response, after several repetitions, as the object or performance actually seen. The nature of the learning process involved, according to this principle, may be represented as follows:

Before Learning New Word or Expression

S (definite stimulus: *evokes a definite response*   R (Reaction: awareness
actual book seen)   or idea of the book)

S' (spoken word: ספר)   R
                        *evokes an indefinite and
                        vague response*

After Learning

S' (spoken word: ספר) by itself *evokes* R (awareness or idea of book)

4. *Multiple Sense Appeal* — Learning a language involves, as was stated above, distinct training in the following abilities: speaking, hearing (understanding the spoken word), reading, and writing. Specific training has to be given in each of these phases. The development of any one does not imply improvement in any of the others. One may be able to understand the language but not to speak it, to read and not to write it, to speak and not to read it, and so on. Unless each of these abilities is specifically learned and connections are established among them, progress in one does not imply progress in the other. Hence, so long as the pupils' interest can be sustained, the linguistic material should be presented through as many senses as possible. This is, moreover, in accord with the psychological principle of facilitation, according to which the effect of combined stimuli calling forth the same response is more certain, prompt, and vigorous.[8] Presenting linguistic material through various sense organs and providing for expression by motor organs in succession heightens the impression and aids in fixing new speech habits. The natural order in learning a language is hearing, pronouncing, seeing (reading), and writing (during the later stages). As soon as the children hear the sentence, phrase, or word, after a few clear repetitions by the teacher, they should be asked to pronounce

[8] Cf. A. I. Gates, *op. cit.*, p. 60 f.; also P. Sandiford, *Educational Psychology*, Longmans, Green and Co., 1929, p. 178.

it. After having heard, learned the meaning of, and pronounced, this word or group of words, the pupils should be shown its "picture" on the blackboard and required to read it. Extensive use should be made of dramatization and acting out. (Refer to Appendix A for further illustrations.)

5. *Multiple Association and Review* — Create and utilize as many natural opportunities and situations as you can for the use of the newly presented sentences, phrases and words. Repetition is most effective only when conducted in many different situations which call forth a variety of responses. Other things being equal, the likelihood that a given fact or word will be remembered is in direct proportion to the number of its associates. The combined power of several associates or "bonds" prevents any obstruction from hindering the recall. In the event that one "bond" disappears temporarily, the other bonds formed will lead to the recall of this one. Furthermore, the varied contexts help to bring out more clearly and definitely the meaning or the different shades of signification of the new word or expression. For example, the word גדול is rendered all the more explicit and meaningful by such varied contexts as אחי הגדול, קול גדול, ספר גדול, כהן גדול, איש גדול, שם גדול, and so on. Various examples drawn from the pupil's experiences, where the use of the particular word or expression may be illustrated, should be provided. Recall context of previous lessons,

in which this word, or another word etymologically related to it, occurred. (See also "Suggestions for Reading Stimuli and Situations," Chap. VII.)

6. *Associating Symbol and Meaning* — The teacher should endeavor to the extent of his resourcefulness to develop in the pupil the ability to comprehend Hebrew materials without the need of passing them through the medium of the native language. Translation, however, cannot be completely discarded. The vernacular image is too strongly imbedded in consciousness to be ignored. It inevitably interposes itself during the initial stages of language learning, and translation takes place either silently or orally. The native equivalents may, therefore, be employed in presenting Hebrew vocabulary, but they should be gradually allowed to sink into the background of consciousness through adequate drill, dramatization, and games. Some of the devices advocated by the exponents of the Direct Method may and should be employed to fix in the mind of the learner the direct connection between symbol and meaning. Among these devices are the following:

a) *Association by Pointing and Gesturing* (showing object, or picture, or acting out) — One of the chief weaknesses of the Translation Method is the fact that it emphasizes abstract verbal memorization rather than sense impressions. Words or concepts are much less easily retained than sense images. The meaning of

הילד הולך for example, is much more abidingly remembered when interpreted concretely by means of a picture or of acting out than by means of native equivalent words. Experimental "evidence points at least to the theoretical advantage of associating the foreign language symbol with objects and activities rather than with words, for promoting learning processes."[9]

b) *Definition and Illustration* — New words can be explained and practiced by familiar expressions and situations, e. g., השב הוא אבי האב או אבי האם. תרח היה השב של יצחק. אברהם היה השב של יעקב ועשו.

c) *Synonyms and Antonyms* — Familiar or partly familiar synonyms and antonyms, or analogous phrases should be recalled in presenting and practicing new vocabulary, e. g.; בלילה חשך — ביום אור; ברא=עשה; שלמה צוחק—שלום בוכה. This calls into play half-forgotten vocabulary, thus serving the purpose of review and testing. Moreover, the thought-kinship of such groups or words serves as an additional association bond, thus aiding in retention. (See above, No. 5, p. 56)

d) *Etymology* — Trace words to simpler or more basal forms, e. g., הולך, ילך, וילך; יצא, יוצא, צא, נצא; etc. This piecemeal examination of words helps to develop language sense and to establish a wide chain

---

[9] R. H. Fife, *A Summary of Reports on the Modern Foreign Languages*, Macmillan, 1931, p. 154.

of association bonds. Linguistic impressions are thereby fixated and made permanent.

e) *Analysis and Synthesis* — Another aid in fixing linguistic material, in consonance with the principles of the "psychological" method, is to group vocabulary around a general category, analyzing the whole into its component parts, or building up the whole from its parts. The analytic procedure is the more effective, since the whole suggests its parts and hints at their respective meanings. Examples: בגן יש עשב, עצים ופרחים. במשפחה יש אב, אם, בן, ובת. בפנים יש מצח, אזנים, עינים, אף, פה וסנטר.

f) *Classroom Directions* — Since the classroom offers natural and varied opportunities for the recurrent use of the vocabulary, it is advisable to incorporate as much of the newly learned vocabulary as possible into classroom directions and activities. The teacher may also create various classroom activities and monitorial functions for which Hebrew expressions can be employed, in order to enlarge the pupils' vocabulary and to create a hebraic atmosphere in the classroom. A list of these classroom expressions will be found in "Appendix B."

g) *Questions and Answers* — The use of simple questions and answers calling for the exercise of the newly learned vocabulary is highly advisable. It provides natural situations for drill and review, and develops facility in speaking and clearness in comprehension of the language. The teacher should, however, take pains to formulate his questions in such a manner as to include the new vocabulary needed for the answer. However, the practice of insisting on complete sentences in the answers is to be discouraged, whenever it makes for artificiality and inhibits natural conversation.

7. *The Unit of Language Is the Sentence* — The word is not to be regarded as the unit of language any more than is the sound. Historically, as well as psychologically, the sentence precedes the word. Individual words, when used by children, or by adults under emotional stress, are really condensed sentences and express a thought-unit implicitly centered about the suggestive word; compare the outcry, "Fire!" "Aeroplane!" and the like. The savage, for example, can hardly be made to name an object without incorporating it into a sentence or bringing it into relation with something else.[10] Illiterate adults are found to have but a very vague notion of the word division in their language, and in their spelling they display the tendency of running together words that should be separated.[11] According to Otto Jespersen, language began with inseparable irregular conglomerations of long strings of syllables. The component elements sub-

---

[10] Cf. A. H. Sayce, *Introduction to the Science of Language*, C Kegan Paul and Co., 1879, p. 120 f.

[11] J. Piaget, *Language of Children*, Harcourt, Brace, 1926, p. 133.

sequently disentangled themselves in the process of the evolution of the language, giving to each element a free existence, and providing devices by which such elements entered into grammatical relations with each other. This may be the reason why in ancient Hebrew manuscripts there was no division, as students of the subject know, of the text into words, phrases or clauses.

In brief, the individual word has an independent existence only for the lexicographer or philologist. In actual life situations the use of isolated words is hardly ever called for. Hence words should never be presented, and should be sparingly practiced, in isolation. A word receives meaning only from context and should be presented and studied in a contextual setting. This applies both to oral work and to reading. In fact, experiments in reading tend to prove that accuracy of recognition increases with the increasing organization of the reading material. Sentences are grasped more quickly than words and the latter more quickly than individual sounds. The total setting, the immediate and remote context in the larger organization unit, all help to make the individual word more meaningful, clearer, richer in associations, and hence more permanent. This is in accord with the principle demonstrated by scientific research and observation, namely, that the learning process of the normal mind proceeds from the general to the particular, and from the whole to its parts. It is, accordingly, better to learn a complicated process as a whole rather than to learn the parts separately and try to combine them later.

8. *Social Atmosphere* — Any language method is effective only in the degree to which it provides for free and easy self-expression. Vocalization and speech are natural responses of children; they should not be stifled but rather directed wisely in accord with the teacher's aim. Any restraint, exertion, or irritation, dries up the powers of self-expression and inhibits learning responses. Create, therefore, a fire-place or playground atmosphere in the classroom. Be *on speaking* rather than *on teaching* terms with your pupils. Let conversation flow easily and naturally. Stimulate and encourage in your pupils the urge to speak, for this is a necessary requisite for learning a language. But *utilize this urge for the presentation and exercise of the desired vocabularies*. Whatever new words and expressions have been learned should, as far as possible, be incorporated in the classroom vocabulary, both for instructional and conversational purposes.

9. *Local Atmosphere* — It is a well known fact that the most effective way of learning a foreign language is to go to the country where it is spoken. But since this is generally impossible, the next best thing is to introduce artificially the environment of that country to the learner, or to transfer him in imagination into that environment and to make him experience vicar-

iously the need of learning the new language, in order to become socialized into this new environment. Children are normally very imaginative and the resourceful teacher will have no difficulty in achieving this end. Progressive language teachers have come to recognize the tenet that a literature, as well as a language, can be taught properly only on a background of a sympathetic knowledge of the people who speak it, of their history, culture, civilization, and institutions. An atmosphere where the speaking of the language is a natural process should be introduced in the classroom by means of illustrative material, maps, signs, lantern slides, posters, pictures, etc.

This is particularly true in the case of the Hebrew language which is not to us merely a "foreign" language, the vehicle of a foreign civilization, culture, etc. A positive element in methods of teaching Hebrew is, therefore, the introduction of a Palestinian or a natural Hebrew-speaking background. It should be complemented, however, by the teacher with all the necessary illustrative aids to make this background rich with experiences and impressions of Jewish life. The walls in the classroom should blaze with Hebrew vocabulary, with reading situations and stimuli, with maps, charts, and pictorial materials. Correspondence with children in Palestine is a very helpful device in this regard. It is through these means that we can hope to implant in the children, early in their lives, a feeling and love for the Hebrew language and to cultivate in them the consciousness of the intimate relationships existing among the Hebrew language, Palestine, and the Jewish people. Teachers of Hebrew may consequently be spared the disheartening questions, asked frequently by older pupils implicitly and explicitly, such as "Why study Hebrew?" "What good will it do me?" "Of what use will it be to me?", etc. In consonance with this principle some modern Hebrew primers such as Scharfstein's *Artzenu*, Rubinstein's *Le-Eretz Yisrael*, Rappaport's *Be-Eretz Yisrael* and the author's *Sippuri I*, operate exclusively with a Palestinian setting.

10. *Dramatization* — So much importance has been attached to dramatization as an educative device in the elementary grades, as to make it deserving of special treatment. One of the outstanding features of a good method is the arrangement of the language material from the very outset in a form which renders it suitable for dramatization. That children regale in dramatizations and make-believe play is obvious to all who had the opportunity to observe children in their free, unrestrained moods. The advantages of dramatization in teaching are numerous and are universally recognized. A leading authority on elementary education states them as follows:

"1. The child's natural love for full bodily expression is utilized in making school life and unpleasant duties less irksome.

PSYCHOLOGICAL PRINCIPLES 65

"2. The more bodily expression we have in school, the less children will suffer through enforced confinement. The dramatic is a step toward a less sedentary program . . .

"3. The natural emotional life of children is given opportunity for proper expression. The feelings are being given more attention in education than heretofore, and, as the basic elements in mental life, they deserve it. There is purification in proper emotional expression, and when children have opportunity for such, they are likely to be more wholesome in their reaction toward the mechanical side of school work and in their lives outside of school.

"4. Facts are better remembered when experienced in this manner. The lesson is expressed more fully than reading and ordinary recitation could bring about; the mind is ready and eager for work; and more repetition under concentrated attention may be demanded. These are special features of economic learning as established by psychological experiments, — full expression by the learner, a slight emotional state to give the attention an edge, and constant repetition.

"5. A motive for special preparation is furnished. The child is to give his interpretation of a chosen piece . . . to his fellows. This brings up a real life situation. Beyond the result in teacher's grade book is the reception of his work by his fellows. This feature alone is full justification for large use of the dramatic.

The more life motives and actual life experience we bring into school the better will be the results of education."[12]

A note of warning should perhaps be sounded in this connection, namely, that unless the teacher can enter wholeheartedly into the spirit of the dramatization and can communicate the enthusiasm to the class, the dramatization is apt to degenerate into a cumbrous, stumbling, and mechanical exercise. Furthermore, no children should be called on to rehearse or perform in front of the class unless they are fairly well prepared. Adequate preparation through seat rehearsals, with the active participation of the entire class in the form of criticisms and suggestions, should, therefore, precede the actual dramatization in front of the class. Each pupil should be encouraged to try out for a certain part and to study his part in preparation for the preliminary class rehearsal. At this rehearsal, the pupils should be given a chance to read or recite their respective parts, and the characters are then chosen by the class. The teacher should not insist on a star performance and should give most of the pupils the opportunity to participate at one time or another in the dramatization. Planning for a dramatization, when wisely directed, is sometimes more beneficial for educational

---

[12] George E. Freeland, *Modern Elementary School Practice*. Revised edition, 1926, Macmillan, p. 159 f

purposes than the actual performance, because of the motives that it may provide for effective drill and review. Dramatization should be an incentive *for*, not a diversion *from*, school work.

QUESTIONS AND EXERCISES

1. Define or explain the following terms or principles in relation to the teaching of Hebrew: Multiple Sense Appeal, Purposeful Activity, Integrated Practice, Specific Practice, Local Atmosphere, Social Atmosphere, Multiple Association and Review, Conditioned Response, Self-Activity.

2. What are some effective ways of presenting vocabulary?

3. What are the advantages of dramatization? What use can be made of it in the teaching of Hebrew? What precautions must be taken in conducting a dramatization?

4. Evaluate the Translation and the Direct Methods in the light of the criteria of language methodology presented in this chapter.

5. Are the following statements valid? Give reasons for your answers. What bearing does your conclusion in each case have on the teaching of Hebrew?

   a. The unit of language is the sentence, not the word.

b. Learning proceeds normally as follows:
   (a.) from the simple to the complex
   (b.) from the known to the unknown
   (c.) from the part to the whole
c. Practice in mechanical reading will not improve ability to read meaningful material.
d. A language can be taught effectively without the use of any oral practice.
e. Young children learn new vocabulary better when presented to the ear than when presented to the eye.
f. It is impossible to eliminate altogether from consciousness the native equivalent of the foreign symbols.
g. A language can be learned effectively by studying each day a list of a few isolated words, supplemented by one or two rules of grammar.
h. It is advisable, in the early stages of learning a language, to present to the pupils misspelled words or incorrect sentences and then to have the pupils correct them.

REFERENCES

The same references as in the preceding chapter. Also recommended are the following references relative to the drill type of lesson:

BURTON, WILLIAM — *The Nature and Direction of Learning*, Appleton, 1929, pp. 343–67.

MORRISON, H. C. — *The Practice of Teaching in the Secondary School*, University of Chicago Press, 1931, Chapter XXVI.
PARKER, S. C. — *General Methods of Teaching*, Ginn, 1919, pp. 247-268.
STORMZAND, M. J. — *Progressive Methods of Teaching*, Houghton, Mifflin, 1929, pp. 149-183.
YOAKAM, G A. AND SIMPSON, R. G. — *An Introduction to Teaching and Learning*, Macmillan, 1935, Chapter X.

Chapter IV

THE PROBLEM OF READING IN THE JEWISH SCHOOL

The Nature of the Problem in General and in Jewish Education

The teaching of reading is regarded as the most troublesome subject in the public elementary school. Indeed, studies of the causes of failure in the elementary grades reveal that deficiencies in reading are almost wholly responsible for these failures in the primary grades and largely responsible for them in the higher grades, the figures ranging from 99% in the first grade to 70% in grade 3 and to 25% in grades 7 and 8. It is accordingly obvious that even in general education, reading is not a problem of the first grade only. It is a problem of the more advanced grades as well. Each grade has reading problems on its own level of difficulty and of a distinctive character. It is, however, true that the reading habits formed during the initial stages of language learning determine the progress of the pupils in their advanced work. Hence, special attention must be devoted in the primary grades to the initiation and cultivation of proper reading habits.

These deficiencies in the teaching of reading still obtain in general education despite the fact that for the past four decades numerous investigations and researches have been carried out in the field of reading, new methods of teaching reading have been tested and improved, and a wealth of ingenious teaching devices and materials has accumulated. How much more serious a problem is, then, the teaching of reading Hebrew in our schools, where the antiquated phonetic method is still predominating and where neither the need nor the urge to come to grips with the problem has, as yet, been seriously felt. It has never been determined to what extent the enormous proportion of retardation and elimination in our schools is attributable to our inefficient reading methods, but that such methods are chiefly responsible for these evils can almost be taken for granted. The emphasis in our curriculum on the mastery of arbitrary signs and meaningless symbols rather than on thought-content does not tend to develop facility and interest in reading. It is significant that in spite of all our efforts and improved techniques and materials, our schools in this country have not succeeded in raising readers of Hebrew literature. It is only by much practice and by steeping ourselves extensively in reading matter that some of us succeeded in overcoming the early disadvantages of inefficient training in reading.

Reading Objectives in the Primary Grades

The assumption so widely prevalent among our teachers, that the reading problem is solved as soon as our pupils have learned to combine synthetically the Hebrew letters and vowels, is certainly baseless. Reading is a process of extracting meaning from the written or printed symbols directly and spontaneously. Ability to combine and pronounce sounds and syllables is not aid to reading; it may even be a hindrance. The practice of viewing reading as an ensemble of syllables and sounds interferes with the development of a reading-attitude, that is, an attitude of approaching the printed or written page with the object of gaining ideas or information therefrom. Witness the large proportion of our pupils who, even when reaching the intermediate or higher grades fail to acquire economic and efficient habits of reading sense-material in Hebrew, whose reading is halting and choppy, and who consequently have no interest in reading Hebrew beyond the assigned tasks.

The chief objectives in the teaching of reading in the primary grades should, therefore, be: (a) to develop economic and efficient habits of reading for meaning; (b) to cultivate a taste and a desire for reading Hebrew; and (c) to train in the ability to attack eventually unfamiliar and *Siddur* material. Pupils should be trained from the outset to extract meaning from the reading material directly, without the conscious interposition of letters and sounds. They should eventually learn to recognize these letters and sounds, but only after they have acquired the habit of looking for meaning in the reading matter, even before it is sounded.

Physiological Basis of Reading

It has been proved conclusively by photographic records of eye-movements that in reading the eye does not move continuously from letter to letter or from sign to sign, but proceeds in a series of rapid, jerky movements, each of them occupying about one-fourtieth of a second. The actual seeing or reading, therefore, does not take place during this quick movement, but during the "fixation pauses," that is, the intervals between one jump and the next, which occupy about 90 percent of the reading time. Consequently, it takes about as much time to read a word or a phrase, depending on the character or the content and on the reader's familiarity with it, as it takes to read a single letter. "Indeed, it is easier and requires less time to read ten words arranged in a meaningful order, than it does to read ten unrelated single letters."[1] For the same reason it is possible to see as many familiar geo-

[1] J. A. O'Brien, *Reading; Its Psychology and Pedagogy*, Century Co., 1926, p. 97

metrical figures, composed of a large number of dots or lines, as single dots or lines. The unity and coherence of meaning helps the eye to sweep, with comprehension, over several words, containing a thought-whole, at a single glance. It has been demonstrated by experimentation that the eye can grasp not only words and phrases, but entire sentences, consisting of as many as seven words, in an almost infinitesimal fraction of a second.[2] The extent of reading matter grasped during the "fixation pauses" varies, of course, with the maturity of the reader and with the ease or familiarity of the reading material. Thus, in learning to read English in American schools, 17 twenty-fifths of a second, the average duration of "fixation pauses" near the beginning of the year, is reduced to 9 twenty-fifths at the end of one year, and to 6 twenty-fifths in grade VI and in later grades.[3] During the "pauses" only parts and general configurations are observed, but these are sufficient to suggest the word or thought-unit as a whole. The past experience and associations of the reader relative to the reading matter, as well as his purpose and the general context, supplement these parts and make them meaningful.

[2] Cf. William A. Smith, *The Reading Process*, Macmillan, 1922, p. 138; also J. A. O'Brien, *Silent Reading*, Macmillan, 1921, p. 3.
[3] See G. T. Buswell, *Fundamental Reading Habits*, University of Chicago, 1922, p. 32.

Furthermore, the natural tendency of the eye movement is in rhythmic sweeps and, in the case of properly trained readers, the eye moves along the printed page with a steady, progressive sequence. It should, therefore, be the object of the teacher of reading to develop those reading habits which are found to be characteristic of efficient readers, namely; (a) a long recognition span, that is, the ability to embrace and recognize large reading units at a single glance, thereby decreasing the number of "fixation pauses" per line; (b) short duration of "fixation pauses," or quick perception of words "fixated" in thought units; (c) regular, rhythmic, and steadily progressive eye-movements; and (d) decreasing vocalization.

Fallacies of the Phonic Method

The general practice in our schools to teach reading by the phonic method and to concentrate attention on the mechanics of reading, even when thought-getting is intended, goes directly counter to those objectives. The eye is narrowed down to a single sound or word, thereby multiplying indefinitely the number of "fixation pauses," producing numerous eye-movements in the reverse direction and causing serious eye-strain. This practice leads inevitably to regressive eye-movements, namely, the backward shifting of the eye, which is detrimental to the establishment of proper reading habits.

Furthermore, the tendency to attack reading matter as a mosaic of syllables and words to be first pronounced, then interpreted into thought units, is not only wasteful but also breeds poor mental habits. Instead of having stimuli (reading matter) result immediately in an ideational response (awareness of the object, act or idea), the first result is a mechanical response of pronunciation, which in turn stimulates the ideational response. The primary reaction of the reader is, thus, the combination of sounds, while thought-getting is a secondary reaction. The learner acquires the idea that the sound is the thing, and this is what he looks for, with the result that there is very little reserve of attention left for comprehension of what is read, or for assimilating it and thinking about it. The edge of thought is certainly blunted by this indirect and involved psychological process, and a situation is created at the outset of the learner's career which is hard to remedy and which results in serious handicaps in reading later on. Evidence of these effects may be found in the halting and choppy reading of meaningful but unfamiliar reading material, which is common even among pupils of our intermediate and advanced grades.

Teachers are, doubtless, acquainted with the fact that quite frequently even advanced pupils experience great difficulty in comprehending the sense of certain Hebrew selections in which they may understand every word separately; while the same pupils, properly trained, "get the thought" of selections in English in which they may miss the meaning of a number of words. The explanation is obvious. The former case is another instance of failing to see the forest because of the trees. "This word is to be pronounced this way, and in that word a letter is indistinct or unfamiliar. This word means this, and that word I forget. This word looks like another word I learned sometime ago, and that I never met." Every element of unfamiliarity or difficulty offers a mental blockade and prevents the spontaneous flashing of meaning. Isolated elements are generally in the foreground of attention and interfere with the reading problem. There is little, if any, reserve of attention left for reacting to meaning.

In the second case, however, the thought content in its totality is central in the mind, while the isolated elements group themselves in their proper places in the whole complex of meaning. Slightly unfamiliar or totally new words are either guessed at from the context, or are passed over for the present until the meaning of the whole passage is grasped. The meaning reaction is primary and instantaneous. Symbols are quickly recognized, clearly apprehended and integrated into a pattern of thought and meaning.

Proper Reading Approach and Its Underlying Principles

Words should be like windows. They should be looked *through* and not *at*. The window may have spots and scratches, or even small opaque segments, but the object looked at is, nevertheless, seen, more or less clearly. The same should be true of words. A word here and there may not be clear or understood, but this should not prevent the getting of the general idea. The purpose in reading should be to grasp the thought, not to observe combination of sounds. The actual process of reading should be automatic and kept in the background of consciousness in order to allow for the concentration of attention in thought-getting. In acquiring any skill, for that matter, the important principle is to give attention to the result rather than to the mechanics of the process. In shooting, for example, one must concentrate on the target rather than on the process. Thought units, consisting either of phrases or short sentences, are, therefore, to be presented to the learner from the very outset, and in the later stages as well, the learner should be guided to direct his attention at the thought-content rather than at the mechanics.

Furthermore, the reading materials should represent ideas and experiences which are familiar to the child. He must be able to draw from his personal experience the meanings which are to be linked to the words and expressions. Thus, in some of our methods, Hebrew phrases and expressions are introduced within the framework of a story-context taken from child-life and told in English. As those linguistic Hebrew elements are presented and explained, their "pictures" are shown on the board or flash-card. The pupils are then asked to read them as whole thought-units. Only after considerable practice in recognizing these thought-units and after the mastery of a fairly large number of sight-words as symbols of meaning, only then are the children taught to analyze the words and to identify the component parts: the words, letters and vowel-signs. (See the following chapter and the lesson plan in Appendix A.)

The Law of Association or Conditioned Response (See preceding chapter) is operative also in this instance. Thus, when an auditory symbol in the native language is presented simultaneously with the related written symbol, the response (ideational or motor) will attach itself to the written or printed symbol, after several repetitions, as readily as to the familiar auditory symbol. Similarly, if after the child has learned adquately the "foreign" spoken symbols, the written equivalents are presented together with, or immediately after, the spoken symbols, the same formation process of new connections will occur as a result of repeated associations and exercise; and the written symbols will arouse the same response as the spoken equivalents. At first the written symbol will evoke the oral impression, and this in turn will call for the idea or meaning. But after some practice the intermediary oral link will disappear, and a direct connection will be established, by a process of short-circuiting, between the written symbol and the meaning. But unless the "foreign" word has become sufficiently familiar and its meaning well established in the mind of the learner, the reaction to the written symbol will be that of pronunciation and not that of meaning. Hence, occasional check-up is necessary to recall the thought context of the unit read.

The phonic method is based on the erroneous assumption that in learning we must proceed from the simple to the complex. But the case is quite the reverse. The normal mind does not naturally learn by observing singly the elemental parts of a complex situation, and by combining them, then, into the whole. On the contrary, both in every-day experience and in classroom learning a straight-away attack is the more natural and the more effective. We are born, in the words of William James,[4] into "one great, blooming, buzzing confusion," and we are confronted, from the very outset, with complex situations. Only as time

---

[4] William James, *The Principles of Psychology*, Henry Holt, 1890, I, 488.

goes on and as our experience grows do we come to analyze the simple elements of these situations.

Piaget concludes,[5] on the basis of extensive experimentation with children, that the reasoning of the child takes place in accordance with a total schema in his mind. The whole is always comprehended and attacked in its totality. Analysis or examination of details comes later and is viewed as a function of the general schema. For example, the reaction to the word *cat* is not the sum total of the reactions to letters *c*, *a*, and *t* in isolation. Nor are the reactions to these individual letters, when viewed as components of the word *cat*, as in the case of learning to spell the word, for example, the same as the reactions to these letters in isolation. The integration, mutual merging, and inter-influence of the letters in the total word has already changed and determined the special character of these letters as symbols of meaning.

What is true of individual letters in relation to the word is true of the individual words in relation to the sentence. Words like sounds are not "things-in-themselves." They have no reality in isolation. It is only by virtue of their context that they acquire significance and signification. United they stand, divided they fall. Hence, in learning to read,

---

[5] J. Piaget, *op. cit*, pp. 132 f. and 155 f.

or, for that matter, in all types of learning, the natural procedure is from the complex to the simple and then back to the complex.

Specific Character of the Problem in the Teaching of Hebrew

In teaching to read a "foreign" language the teacher is obviously confronted with a problem entirely different from that of teaching to read a native tongue. In the latter case the child generally comes to his primary grade equipped with a vocabulary of several thousand words, on which the teacher can base his reading exercises. In the former instance, however, the task of the teacher is to provide and develop a vocabulary background in the foreign language, by means of oral and written exercises and drill. The living voice of the teacher, with the aid of the blackboard, has to be employed in place of the textbook in the initial stages of foreign language learning. Before the child gets to the reading of the lesson in the textbook, the vocabulary and the written symbols should have become sufficiently familiar by dint of practice to make the reading in the book an intelligible and truly delightful exercise. It is in this manner only that a correct reading attitude can be built up.

Effective technique in methods of teaching reading will doubtless result in more efficient reading habits.

But just here the real task of the Jewish primary teacher begins. It is not only our aim to enable our pupils to read with facility and understanding, but more particularly to make our children like to read, to arouse and stimulate in them reading interests and a taste for good books; in brief, to enable and predispose them to read widely and to read wisely. "That schooling which results in this taste for good reading, however unsystematic or eccentric this schooling may have been, has achieved a main end of elementary education; and that schooling which does not result in implanting this permanent taste has failed. Guided and animated by this impulse to acquire knowledge and exercise his imagination through reading, the individual will continue to educate himself all through life. Without that deep-rooted impression he will soon cease to draw on the accumulated wisdom of the past and the new resources of the present, and as he grows older he will live in a mental atmosphere which is always growing thinner and emptier... The uplifting of the democratic masses depends upon this implanting at school of a taste for good reading."[6]

In the field of general education, reading may no longer provide the sole key, although still certainly the most potent and most significant, to the social and cultural heritage of a people. So many other mediums

---

[6] Charles Eliot, quoted by G. E. Freedland's *op cit.*, p. 147 f.

of learning and experiencing are available in the modern environment, which furnish stimulation and guidance and may sometime make up for the deficiencies of formal education, such as the radio, the movies, the pictorial magazines, forums, lectures and other environmental factors. But there can hardly be any question as to the poignancy of Eliot's statement when applied to Jewish schooling in this country. It is an irrefutable and painful fact that the Jewish American environment is, as yet, inane and barren of opportunities for genuine Jewish experiencing and learning. Jewish experiences and values are deposited primarily in literary forms of expression rather than in existing practices and institutions. In order, therefore, to bring our pupils into possession of these experiences and values we have no other effective means than that of immersing them gradually and progressively in the rich deposits stored away in our Hebrew literature. It is only through such avenues that we can restore for our children the glories of the past, bring into bold relief the significant aspects of the present, and keep before them the vision of the ideal as a beacon for the future.

Thus training in the ability to read Hebrew with understanding and appreciation, fostering habits and desires to read Hebrew, and the cultivation of tastes for good Hebrew reading-matter must constitute the ultimate aim in teaching Hebrew in the Jewish weekday school. Beginning with our primary grades, our efforts in the teaching of Hebrew should be directed toward building up in our children the abilities, habits and desires, which may eventuate in a continuous and growing interest in reading Hebrew. This reading will serve as the open sesame to the literary treasures of Judaism, undiluted by paraphrases and unadulterated by translations. Through such reading our pupil will come to identify himself with the experiences, struggles, aspirations, sufferings and joys of our people throughout all times and all climes. His own life will, in consequence, be expanded, deepened and enriched. He will envisage the world and events about him more clearly, and he will feel about them more keenly.

In Summary

To sum up, the objectives in the teaching of reading in the primary grades are as follows:

1. To introduce reading as a thought-getting process. Children should be made to realize that reading is a means of gaining thoughts, ideas and experiences. They should be trained to look for meaning in all written or printed matter.

2. To inculcate, as a first step in reading, the knowledge and immediate recognition of a number of sight-words.

3. To develop the ability to recognize unfamiliar words independently by means of phonetic training.

4. To cultivate proper physiological reading habits, such as long eye-span, short fixation pauses, rhythmic and progressive eye-movements, right-to-left eye-sweeps, and accurate return-sweeps of the eye from the end of the line to the beginning of the next.

5. To foster tastes in reading and to train in the habit of reading thoughtfully, critically and appreciatively.

QUESTIONS AND EXERCISES

1. Define the following terms: reading, fixation pause, regressive eye-movements, phonic method, recognition span, thought-unit.

2. Is learning to read, a problem of the first grade only? What is the available evidence in this regard in the field of general education? What indirect evidence may be adduced in the teaching of Hebrew?

3. What are the objectives in the teaching of Hebrew in the primary grades?

4. How does the good reader differ from the poor reader in terms of eye-movements and reading attitude?

5. What are the weaknesses of teaching reading by the phonic method? What evidence of these weaknesses may be adduced from our observation and experience in the teaching of Hebrew?

6. How can the teaching of reading Hebrew be improved in the light of eye-movement studies?

7. What other experimental and theoretical evidence is there, outside of eye-movement studies, in support of teaching reading by thought-units rather than by sounds?

8. In what respect does the problem of teaching our children in this country reading of Hebrew differ from that of teaching them English? How can the disadvantages in the case of Hebrew be overcome?

9. What is the ultimate aim in teaching the reading of a language?

10. Why is the effective teaching of reading of such great pedagogic value in the field of general education and of even greater value in that of Jewish education?

11. In the light of the principles underlying efficient reading habits, criticize the type of children's literature, which is too densely vocabularized, or which is interspersed too thickly, within the text, with translations.

REFERENCES

BROOKS, F. D. — *The Applied Psychology of Reading*, Appleton, pp. 26–84.
BUSWELL, G. T — *Fundamental Reading Habits*, University of Chicago Press, pp. 11–57.
——— *A Laboratory Study of the Reading of Modern Foreign Languages*, Macmillan.

GATES, A. I. — *The Improvement of Reading*, Revised Edition, Macmillan, Chapters I and II.
——— *Psychology of Reading and Spelling*, Teachers College, Columbia University.
HUEY, E. B. — *The Psychology and Pedagogy of Reading*, pp. 1–185.
JUDD, C. H. AND BUSWELL, G. T. — *Silent Reading*, University of Chicago Press.
KLAPPER, P. — *Teaching Children to Read*, Revised Edition, Appleton, Chapters I–VII.
O'BRIEN, J. A. — *Reading, Its Psychology and Pedagogy*, Century, pp. 1–114, pp. 141–164.
PARKER, S. C. — *Types of Elementary Teaching and Learning*, Ginn, Chapters V, VI, XI.
SMITH, W. A. — *The Reading Process*, Macmillan, pp. 1–20, 88–150.

Chapter V

THE CHOICE AND USE OF TEXT AND READING MATERIALS IN HEBREW

In the light of the discussion in the preceding chapter, it should be clear that the textbook and reading materials used in the teaching of Hebrew play a very important role, especially in the primary grades. A wise choice will lead to the achievement of the reading objectives listed above; an unwise choice will have the contrary effect. A great deal of care and deliberation should, therefore, be exercised in choosing these materials, and objective, scientifically established criteria should be employed for this purpose.

Choice of Vocabulary

In the first place these materials should be selected with the view to equipping our pupils in the primary grades adequately for the study of those selections from the Bible and from modern Hebrew literature which are generally included in the curriculum of our elementary grades. During these preparatory stages an effort must be made to unload the vocabulary burden of these classical selections, so that they may be studied, in due course of time, with comparative ease and with particular emphasis on the understanding and appreciation of content and style. Hence, the primary reading materials should operate with vocabularies which occur with a high rate of frequency in the classical selections and should incorporate a high degree of recurrence-frequency of these vocabularies. In the final analysis, the more often a word or expression is seen in a natural reading context, the more effectively it is learned for reading purposes, without the need of resorting to any extrinsic devices of drill and practice. This is, after all, the most "natural method" of learning a language with a reading objective. A certain number of vocabulary studies are now available which will be helpful to the teacher in this regard and to which reference will be made in a subsequent chapter.

The vocabulary of primary reading materials should, of course, be simple, that is, it should deal with concepts and ideas which are within the experience of the children. It should, however, be bookish rather than conversational. Grammatical and idiomatic peculiarities, which are characteristic of the classical texts and are there of common occurrence, must be transmitted gradually and systematically to our pupils during the preparatory stages, or they will find these language difficulties overwhelming and perhaps insurmountable when they are plunged into the study of these texts. Obviously, the vocabulary load must be thinly and evenly distributed, in order to avoid overtaxing them with too many words at a time.

Interesting Content

Interesting content is manifestly an essential requisite in children's reading matter. The first lessons will, of necessity, have to be confined within a limited framework of vocabulary and of content. The use of English may be resorted to, in presenting these lessons, in order to widen the narrative scope and to provide needed supplementary details.[1] As the children's vocabulary increases, the amount of English supplementation should proportionately decrease. The normal child in our elementary grades resents being babied and fed on small infantile doses of scrappy and trivial reading matter, such as is characteristic of many of our readers in the elementary grades. He wants a real story, with full-blooded characters, lots of action, adventure, and so on. Furthermore, he wants to have the printed pages tell him something he wants to know, rather than to have them serve as an "excuse" for learning vocabulary.

[1] See "Type Lesson Plan," Appendix A.

Children's Reading Interests

The reading interests of children have been a subject of extensive investigation in the field of general education over a period of may years, but without achieving any conclusive evidence. At the present stage, students of this problem admit the inadequacy and incompleteness of these studies for purposes of guidance. Dr. Lois Meek of Columbia University reports, on the basis of her investigations, that "Girls were more interested in plays and stories about 'life today' than were boys, but neither sex cared much for depictions of contemporary life. It was not until the child reached the age of 13 that he or she expressed any real liking for such depictions at all."[2]

Apparently, young children prefer reading material which allows them free scope for imaginative play. They have not yet had, at this tender age, enough direct experience to clip the wings of their imagination and to force them down to a world of realities. George S. Counts is quoted by Paul Witty to the effect that "As a matter of fact, children's interests are potentially as many as the activities of mankind, as varied as the pattern of human culture, and almost as fluid as the passing fashions." In commenting on this statement, Professor Witty observes: "In other words, interests are largely acquired, but their cultivation is one of the

[2] Reported in *The New York Times*, October 8, 1936.

chief functions of education. It is clear, therefore, that consideration of and respect for children's interests need not lead the teacher to abrogate his primary responsibility for influencing and guiding children's growth."[3]

Content of Hebrew Textbook and Reading Matter

In planning materials and methods for our pupils, we should, accordingly, not aim to cater to their transient needs and passing fancies. We should rather endeavor to utilize their present interests as incentives and sources of motivation for the achievement of purposes set up by our educational program. This program should take cognizance of our child as a growing, adapting and changing organism in a changing world. Our child's world, to a much greater degree than the world of the non-Jewish child, extends beyond geographical, cultural, and temporal barriers, and is particularly freighted with problems of adjustment and readjustment. The fate of the Jews in the ghettos of Europe, the birth pains of the new regenerated life in Palestine, problems of resettlement and rehabilitation of Jewish refugees and dispossessed all over the world, all these are constituent elements of his world. Our program must provide for all this and must assume the respon-

[3] *Educational Administration and Supervision*, April, 1938.

sibility for the growth, orientation and integration of the Jewish personality of our children. It must embrace the whole constellation of their interests and needs as Jews, as members of a cultural and religious minority group the world over.

The reading and text materials should, accordingly, be calculated to impart to our pupils significant and varied Jewish content. Types of content which the child generally finds in reading selections in English and which are of general non-Jewish character should, as far as possible, be avoided. On the other hand, our selections should deal with distinctly Jewish content and should, at the same time, endeavor to meet the whole gamut of the pupils' interests, such as stories and depictions of Jewish life in America and in many lands, folklore and legends, biographies and historical narrations, Jewish humor, stories and accounts of Jewish life and achievements in modern Palestine, and so on. Our children should be trained to feel that in order to get certain Jewish information, ideas or experiences, they have to turn to the Hebrew book.

The time available for the study of our language and our literature is scant, and the material to be studied is vast. It is only by utilizing this time most economically and most efficiently that we can hope to achieve some of the major objectives in Jewish education.

There are other requisites for textbook materials in the primary grades which deserve consideration, such as the number and quality of illustrations, the nature and size of the type, the durability and appearance of the paper, and so on. But all these have become so standardized in our primary textbook, as to make the discussion of these times almost superfluous.

Learning to Read vs. Reading to Learn

The process of learning a new language with a reading objective consists of five stages: (1) Associating meaning with oral symbols, words and expressions; (2) attaching meaning to the written or printed symbols; (3) extracting meaning from these symbols and responding to them; (4) cultivating the habit of reading the language and interests in books written in it; and (5) developing desirable tastes and standards and the power of appreciating good literature in that language. The first three stages may be designated as *learning to read*; the last two, as *reading to learn*. The first three stages are within the province of the primary grades and are merely the means to the fourth and fifth stages as the end. Without achieving the end, the efforts invested in attaining the means are largely futile and barren of any real educational value, since they lack, what Dewey regards as the criterion for all educational activity, *growth* or *experiential continuity*. The situation may be compared to that of climbing a mountain and stopping somewhere on the slope before reaching the top. The result is gradual sliding downward until the bottom is reached once again.

Unfortunately the stage of *learning to read* lingers on in our Hebrew schools beyond the primary grades, and even predominates in the advanced grades. Whether we teach Bible or selections from modern Hebrew literature the emphasis is on language learning and on grinding out vocabularies. The teacher generally monopolizes the center of the stage, ladling out information, explaining, drilling and manipulating all the teaching activities. We do not allow our pupils to *learn* because we are too busy *teaching* them. Like the over-solicitous mother we shy from relinquishing our control over our pupils, and we dictate and direct vigilantly every step in the learning process, with the result that our pupils fail to develop a sense of curiosity, initiative, and independence, essential to real learning and growth. The Hebrew book is associated in the minds of our pupils with laborious explanations, word-study, and practice exercises; and one does not turn to a practice book with an attitude of joyful anticipation and of seeking satisfaction for his curiosity or esthetic urges.

Furthermore, the fluency essential to enjoyment and interest in reading cannot come from textbook study or reading, where the many unfamiliar or difficult words necessitate numerous fixations and regressive eye-movements per line. This is especially true in the case of oral reading which is generally in vogue in our schools. The complex muscular process of oral utterance drains away much of the attention needed for comprehension of meaning. The result is a vicious circle. Poor reading habits produced by this type of reading leads to a general dislike of all reading.

In brief, we must break away, in the teaching of Hebrew, from verbalism, from the practice of "learning to read." We should, instead, concentrate our attention on training our pupils in the ability of "reading to learn," especially in the grades above the primary.

Procedure and Nature of the Reading Program and Character of the Materials

Specifically, how will the procedure of training children in *reading-to-learn* differ from that by which they *learn-to-read*? In the former procedure, the teacher is not a drill master, occupying the center of the stage and doing most of the talking and explaining. He keeps himself in the background, as it were, stimulating and guiding the learning process. The pupils will be actively busy reading silently materials, properly graded, from which they will be gleaning information and ideas, in which curiosity and interest has been aroused. The pupils will, of course, be encouraged to take some of these materials to read at home or outside of class. The selections will consist of various types in harmony with the varied range of the children's potential interests which we aim to cultivate. For this purpose, selections from Hebrew literature, such as have stood the test of time because of their inherent literary and educational values, should be mainly utilized. These selections should be adapted within the framework of scientifically graded vocabulary levels, as well of gradually lengthening units, so that the pupils may progress step by step from one level to the next, with consequent growth in language power, in reading interest, and in informational background.

The problem of homogeneous grading of pupils is a difficult one even in the public schools, where the chronological age-level is more or less constant. It is doubly difficult in the Jewish school, where children of varied age-levels and backgrounds must often be kept in the same grade. But by a program such as this the difficulties may be eased, since the subject matter will be graded. Pupils in the same grade, with a relatively wide range in background and capacity, may find material suited to their respective levels. The grading will be in terms of content, vocabulary-range and size of reading unit. After completing one unit, or pamphlet, they will proceed to the next. Some will complete one unit during the class period, others may complete two or three. As a rule, the materials should be read in the class, and permission to take them home should be granted only after sufficient interest in independent reading has been aroused. Oral comments should, as far as possible, be elicited, but excursions into irrelevant discussions in English should be avoided. Some written comments should also be encouraged, such as based on the following questions: Did you like the story? Why? What characters or incidents did you like particularly? Why? Who is the main hero in the story? Would you like to read more stories like this one? Would you prefer stories of a different kind? What kind? and so on.

In order to discourage dawdling and to stimulate rapid reading, a reading chart for each pupil may be kept, recording each day the number of pages read within a given time. The rate of gain should be recorded and stressed.

The teacher's function in this program is to fit the materials to the levels of language and interests of the respective pupils, to stimulate and motivate the reading, to assist and to check on comprehension and on assimilation of the materials. The degree of the teacher's assistance will vary from pupil to pupil and from grade to grade, until it may be entirely dispensed with. Teachers must come to realize that the best teaching is done not when the teacher occupies the center of the stage, holding forth, firing questions and comments; but rather when he stays in the background, as it were, but stimulates and guides the work of his pupils. The class time belongs to the pupils and the teacher has no right to usurp it.

Children, to be sure, do not like to learn in isolation, nor is it desirable to have them isolated for any length of time, since they may develop thereby serious social repressions. Hence, provisions will be made for group activities in such a program. These will consist chiefly of class discussions and reports on reading, of dramatic and festival projects, of singing, as well as of oral reading of such selections as the teacher or the pupils, under the teacher's stimulation, choose to reread aloud, or of such materials as need more intensive treatment, as in the case of poems and difficult biblical passages. But the major part of the time will be devoted to such activities as tend to *liberate the pupils progressively from dependence on the teacher's explanations and proddings and to develop curiosity, initiative, independence, and resourcefulness.*

Such a program postulates, of course, the need of making available abundant and varied reading materials within the limits of the respective vocabulary levels, as well as of making provision for systematic training in independent reading. The *Sifriyah La-No'ar* project (See Chapter IX) is a step in this direction. Eventually, by such a process, our pupils will reach the stage when they will be ready and able to attack literary materials in the original with appreciation and intelligence.

CHAPTER VI

SPECIFIC SUGGESTIONS FOR THE DEVELOPMENT OF PROPER READING HABITS AND ATTITUDES IN THE PRIMARY GRADES

GENERAL CONSIDERATIONS

One of the chief objectives in the teaching of Hebrew in the primary grades, as has been repeatedly stressed here, is the development of a *proper reading attitude* in our pupils. It is not sufficient to have them acquire the ability to read. They must also learn to approach the printed page with the correct attitude, namely, that of gaining from it ideas and information, in which an interest has been aroused; and not one of combining sounds and words, to be pronounced and then to be retraced for the purpose of getting meaning. The pupils should be trained at the outset to extract the meaning directly as they see the words. Reading should be made for them a delightful experience, which stimulates in them the desire to continue and to grow in the power of this ability.

Careful investigations have demonstrated the frequent absence of visual imagery in the reading of many people. This is true of reading in a native language; it is particularly true in the case of reading in a new language. Children may often read and even translate, or tell the meaning of the words read, without having a mental picture of the ideas, information, or acts represented by these words. This is especially noticeable in the case of oral reading, where the reader's attention is drained away by the burdensome and complex process of oral utterance, which interferes seriously with rapid comprehension of meaning. In the effort to achieve accuracy in pronunciation, the thought or content is often neglected. Reading may thus become a motor instead of a comprehension activity. Teachers should guard against such undesirable and wasteful reading habits.

One of the most effective means of vitalizing the drill process and of arousing the children to top-notch effort is the game. Few, if any, devices are capable of calling forth such vivid attention and such gripping interest as a game well played. Under its spell children will work with redoubled zeal and energy. Childhood is the playtime of life, and all normal children, young and older, manifest a wholesome interest in play and competitive games. Alert-minded teachers, especially in the primary grades, recognize this fact and resort to games extensively. A teacher who cannot avail herself of this device is not qualified to teach primary grades.

In order, however, to render the game most effective

SPECIFIC SUGGESTIONS 103

for vocabulary and drill purposes, the following conditions must be satisfied:

1. The game must be carefully chosen by the teacher and modified with the view to meeting the particular needs of her class, as well as the individual differences in the ages, abilities and interests of the pupils.

2. The teacher must enter into the spirit of the game and must become "enthused" over it. She must play *with the children*, and not merely *watch* them play and *direct* the game. A game poorly played is a perfunctory and tedious exercise — a waste of time and educational opportunity.

3. The sentence idea in language games should be developed and emphasized whenever possible. In word and phrase games, the context should be frequently recalled, and an attempt should be made to allow for the words and phrases to group themselves into sentences.

4. In games for vocabulary and sense-reading, the thought content should be analyzed before playing the games. Check up on meaning from time to time. Do not allow the practice to degenerate into parrot-like repetition of meaningless sounds.

5. As far as possible, Hebrew should be employed for giving directions and other incidental expressions in connection with the games.

6. Vary your games. Do not confine yourself to one particular game ad nauseam. There are plenty to

choose from. Treat your pupils to a new game as soon as you see the interest in the old one begin to flag.

7. Do not allow any haggling over scores. Let the rules of the game be clear and definite, and no time should be wasted on extraneous bickering.

8. Encourage cooperative games and activities. The urge for competition is too strongly imbedded and widespread among our children, and it is both futile and unwise to suppress it. Rather take cognizance of it and endeavor to sublimate and direct it into cooperative channels. Create and utilize opportunities for cooperative behavior and reduce to a minimum competitive efforts.

The teacher must also be warned to the effect that games and devices are no substitutes for carefully planned teaching. It cannot be repeated too often that there are no fixed and finished techniques which will suffice for the ever-changing conditions of growth in the pupils and for the varying environmental situations. Children differ from class to class and among themselves. They also differ from day to day, and so do the teachers and the teaching conditions. Games and devices employed effectively with one group of children, under one set of circumstances, may prove entirely unsatisfactory with another group, or even with the same group of children, under a different set of circumstances. Teaching must never become a routine task, a rule of thumb procedure; it must be a dynamic

SPECIFIC SUGGESTIONS 105

process of adjusting the child to an ever-increasing background of experience. It is in the light of this principle that techniques and devices should be selected and operated.

The following procedure and devices are recommended in connection with the use of the Hebrew textbook and other reading materials. Choose the devices which meet the needs of the particular class, content, and situation.

General Procedure

1. Do not expect your primary pupils to "keep the place," or to hold their eyes glued to the page, for any length of time, while somebody reads aloud. The eye-movements involved in reading require a fine degree of motor coordination, and the practice of keeping the eye glued to the line or page in the book, without giving the frail eye-muscles frequent opportunity to relax, is bound to result in disintegration of nerve tissue and in injurious physical and mental strain. Young children should, therefore, be allowed to have their reading practice in the book alternate frequently with activities calling for looking away from the book.

2. The reading exercise should be carried on in a *real audience situation*. The pupils should be impressed with the responsibility of making themselves clearly understood by their "audience." They should be suf-

ficiently prepared to evoke by their reading pleasure and appreciation on the part of the listeners. They should, therefore, be asked to read with a "big" voice, with proper emphasis and intonation, in a conversational way, etc. The "audience," on the other hand, should be made to feel the responsibility of listening courteously, intelligently and critically. Comments and corrections should come from the "audience," of which the teacher is an alert and active "member," who may *sometimes* have the final word in the matter. The teacher should therefore refrain, as a rule, from repeating answers or comments made by the pupils.

3. Plenty of oral and blackboard drill and exercises in the vocabulary of the lesson, emphasizing both the visual and auditory forms, should precede the reading lesson. But, as far as possible, the whole story or content of the lesson should not be given away during the preparatory drill process. Occasionally, the teacher may find it advisable to read the lesson first, in its entirety or in parts, interspersing brief explanations and comments. But the reading in the book by the children should be a smooth-running, uninterrupted activity. No tedium, which might be entailed by drill, should be allowed to associate itself with the book. The teacher should be on guard against allowing reading to degenerate into mere glib word-calling. Whenever this tendency is detected as in the case of the halting sound-by-sound or word-by-word reading, the

pupils should be prompted to read silently first to get the thought before reading orally.

4. In the more advanced grades, the pupils should be trained to read the lesson silently after it has been properly motivated and linguistic difficulties explained and removed. Occasionally, interpretive reading of the selection by the teacher should precede the silent reading by the class. Questions testing comprehension should follow this reading.

5. Translation should be used sparingly during the practice and reading. Whenever possible, recall of familiar context, etymological relationship, or clear illustration should be employed to solve vocabulary difficulties. But incidental translation, if found most economical and effective to remove these difficulties, should not be withheld. Clearness of association between symbol and meaning is basic to proper reading. But as was previously emphasized here, translation should be employed only in presenting vocabulary, but should be discarded or reduced to a minimum in practice activities.

6. Efficient reading is possible only when it is properly motivated. Aimless reading is susceptible to all sorts of distractions and interruptions, while a strong purpose or incentive will impel the reader to "push on" and ignore all such distractions and obstacles. The following may serve as sources of motivation for reading: to find out the end of the story, or what certain

characters said or did; to carry out instructions or directions; to find parts or scenes that can be dramatized or acted out; to answer stimulating questions; to find information that piques the curiosity; etc. In more advanced stages, the pupils should be trained to look for the central thought of the selection read, to outline, organize, or reproduce as many ideas as possible gained from the reading.

Specific Devices and Games

1. Use flashcards for short exposure exercises. They should be flashed rapidly enough to compel the pupil to take in the entire phrase in a glance instead of reading one word at a time. The flashcards may either be connected with the lesson or may contain instructions, such as the following: פתחו את הספרים, סגרו את הספרים, סגור את הדלת, פתח את הדלת, שבו ישר.

2. Practice and encourage pupils to practice phrasing by sounding or underlining words constituting a natural thought unit or closely connected in meaning. In connected sentences underline alternate phrases for example: שם הילד שמואל. הילד הולך אל בית־הספר, etc.

3. Label objects in the room, such as windows, table, blackboard, etc. Take labels off after class and have children replace them the following day.

4. Have a list of cards or labels on which certain

SPECIFIC SUGGESTIONS

directions or words are given. As the teacher or pupil exposes the card, the pupils should be asked, in turn, to indicate comprehension of the word or expression by executing the direction or by acting out, illustrating, drawing or pointing to the object, as the case may be. For example, the pupil stands up, walks over to the blackboard, pretends to be eating, points to the door, etc., all in accord with the words or expressions on the card.

5. Have a list of words or sentences on the board with numbers attached to them. Read or have a pupil read one or more of these reading-units, and one of the pupils give the corresponding number or numbers and read the unit or combination of units to which these numbers are attached.

6. Have a list of words or sentences on the board arranged as in the preceding exercises. Have one child step out of the room while another child selects one of the sentences. Let the child come back into the room and guess which sentence has been selected, saying, "Was it number 4?" (Reading it) and the class answers לֹא, לֹא הָיָה or כֵּן, הָיָה .... (Reading No. 4); etc.

7. Flash a word or phrase-card and call on a child to read it. If he does not read it correctly give him the card, tell him how to read it, and call on him later to read it again. Similarly in blackboard or prayer-book reading, each child should be asked to keep a

list of words misread by him, to be taken up later for special study.

8. Whisper a sentence, phrase, or word, or have a pupil do it. Then have children guess and read this reading unit on the board or in the book by watching carefully the movement of the lips. (This and the following game are particularly effective since they emphasize motor learning which is so helpful in fixing impressions lastingly.)

9. Have a child step out of the room. Let the class decide to trace in the air a word or a line on the blackboard. Call the child in and have him guess the word or the line by watching (from behind) one or more of the children tracing it in the air. See that tracing is done in unison and accurately so as not to be confusing.

10. Sketch a brook with stones in it. Place words on stones, and let children see who can cross the brook, by reading correctly, without "falling into the water."

11. Teacher holds a package of word-cards in her hand. She calls upon the pupils, in turn, to read the exposed card. The pupil who can read the card gets it. Teacher goes up and down the classroom until the package of cards is exhausted. The pupil who has the largest number of cards wins.

12. Draw a ladder on the blackboard. Put a word on each rung, choosing easier words for the bottom and harder words for the top. Call upon one child at

SPECIFIC SUGGESTIONS

a time to "climb the ladder" by reading the words. Let each child go as far as he can. Some of the brighter children might "lend a hand" occasionally and help the weaker ones reach the top. Call upon several children in turn to repeat the performance unaided.

13. Draw a tree with apples on it. Write words on the apples. See how many apples you can pick.

14. Write a column of words. Call on one child at a time to say a word; if he knows it, draw a stone for a wall. See how high a wall can be built.

15. The Goose Pen — The teacher flashes a card to children in turn. The one who misses his card is a goose and goes into the "pen" (some corner or place in the room). The "goose" stays in the "pen" until he "catches" someone by pronouncing a word correctly before the one called upon has time to answer. The latter then goes into the "pen."

16. Playing Store — A number of flashcards, including word and phrase cards, are placed on the blackboard ledge or wherever they can be conveniently exhibited. The teacher or a pupil is the storekeeper. Children come up in turns to buy cards. They say אני חפץ לקנות (reading the card). Ability to read card entitles the buyer to a card, and the "storekeeper" gives him the card saying הנה .... (reading the card sold). At the end of the game the storekeeper or the teacher calls back the cards by reading them and having the pupils come up in turn with their cards,

which they display to the class and have the class read them. The game may also be varied by having the buyer give the meaning of the words or sentences he wishes to purchase.

17. Have several sentences on the board. Have a number of individual word cards which contain all the words needed to build up the sentences on the board. Have the children build up these sentences by means of word cards and have them arrange the cards so that each card will correspond to the word written directly above it on the board. Let them read each word card as they use it.

18. Distribute word cards giving one word to each child. Call a phrase (אל הבית) or a sentence (הילד הולך ברגלים). The children who have these words go to the front of the room and stand in correct order to form the phrase or sentence.

19. Tell, or have a child tell, what a sentence on the board or in the book tells or describes and have another child find and read.

20. Give out cards corresponding to a story written on the board. Have the child with a card like the first sentence come out, then the second one, etc., until the story is completed. This may be varied by having the teacher tell the story (using Hebrew or English context), and as soon as a Hebrew word or sentence is introduced, the pupil with the corresponding card comes to the front of the room. Cards may be called

back by either the teacher or by the pupils by the same procedure.

21. Deaf and Dumb — Children and teacher make believe that they cannot talk. Instead of telling one another to do certain things, they point to a list of action words or sentences on the board and see how fast the instructions can be executed. This list would include such directions as: לך אל הלוח, כתוב על הלוח, פתחו את הספרים, שב על הכסא, סגור את הדלת.

22. Have a list of numbered words or sentences on the blackboard. Divide the class into teams. Give or have a pupil give the English equivalent of one of the words or sentences. Then call on a member of each team to give the number of the Hebrew equivalent and read it. The pupil who finds and reads the Hebrew equivalent first gets a score for his team. Have the other pupil also read the word or sentence.

23. Select in your lesson a number of words on which you may want to drill. Write them on the board in their natural sentence context. Tell the class that one of these words will be erased while they keep their eyes closed. Proceed accordingly. Have them open their eyes, then find the missing word and write it back where it belongs. Use Hebrew directions: סגרו את העינים, פתחו את העינים.

24. A variant of the preceding game is to have one pupil step out of the room. The class decides under the teacher's guidance on a certain word to be erased,

thus having their attention focused on it. The pupil is then called in and asked to find and write back the missing word. The missing words may be written on another side of the blackboard in a random order. The children are then asked in turn to put these words back where they belong.

25. Have a list of key-words or expressions on the board taken from a selection studied. Have pupils build up the selection cooperatively by using these words and expressions in their proper context.

26. Have pupils read in turn a selection from the textbook with proper expression to the class. The class is to attend carefully with their books closed. After each pupil finishes reading the part assigned to him, the class is tested on the contents by asking for the meaning either in English or in Hebrew, or by having them answer questions covered by the portion read. This challenges interpretative reading and close attention.

27. Have a list of Hebrew sentences or expressions on the blackboard. Call on one of the children to come forward, stand up facing the class — his back to the blackboard. Have pupils give, in turn, the English translation of these sentences or expressions which the child standing in front of the class is to translate back into Hebrew without looking at the board.

28. Ask the children to match and read, individually

and occasionally in concert, the sentences and the phrases in the book with those on the blackboard or on flash-cards and labels. The children should be asked either to give the number of the line in which the expression occurs, or to read the whole line.

29. Have pupils, in turn, find and read in the book the part that says ... (giving the meaning in English, when necessary, or conveying it by means of illustration, acting out, etc.)

30. Ask your pupils to read a sentence, or a group of sentences. Then, *looking away from the book*, have them tell you the meaning either in Hebrew (using the same words or different words) or in English. The former is, of course, preferable after the children have acquired sufficient mastery of the vocabulary. There is experimental evidence to prove the superiority of this device over that of studying by rereading repeatedly. It strengthens recall and provides training in silent reading.

31. As a variation of the preceding device have one child read, with proper expression, a group of sentences or a paragraph representing a thought unit. Then call on one of the children to repeat it in the same or synonymous vocabulary by looking away from the book.

32. Have children select parts to be acted out, in turn, individually or in groups, then have the class find and read the parts acted out. The teacher should

help make the acting out really interpretative and meaningful.

33. Distribute labels or cards, containing beginnings and endings of sentences, or questions and answers. Give one group, or team, the "beginnings" or questions, and another the "endings" or answers. Call upon members of one team to read in turn their labels and have the members of the other team read, in their turn, the corresponding endings and answers. Then have children pass their cards around, to the left or to the right, and proceed in the same manner, in order to give each child a chance to read and to match as many of these labels as possible.

34. Have a number of word- or phrase-cards, constituting a story, or the "key" expressions of the story, distributed among the children. Have them look in their books, and as they read a line or a group of lines, those children having the words or phrases read, come forward and arrange their cards on the ledge of the board. Proceed in this manner until the selection or the story is built up. Children coming up with their cards show them to the class, and the class reads them singly and in thought units.

35. Let the teacher, or preferably a pupil, read a group of words, representing thought units, in the book, and have members of the class find it, read it, and explain it.

36. Have the pupils read in the book the part which

describes what a certain picture represents or what a certain character says or does.

37. Read, or have a pupil read, with expression, a certain selection from the book, while the class is listening, looking away from the books. Pause at certain suggestive spots and have pupils tell you the word or words that follow, either by looking into the book and finding the place, or from memory. These words may also be listed on the blackboard in a random order, as an aid to the pupils.

38. Select a number of conspicuous phrases or sentences. Arrange them in a random order. Have them rearranged in the proper order by using the guidance of the text-book, or from memory of content.

39. Have a list of questions on the board, or ask them orally in turn, and have the class find the sentence or group of sentences which answers these questions.

40. Plan and prepare a dramatization. Tell your children that a preliminary rehearsal will be held the next day, or the day after, when the characters will be selected. Each pupil should be encouraged to try out for a certain part and to study this part at home. At the preliminary rehearsal each pupil (excepting of course the slowest and most incapable) should be given a chance to read or recite his part, and the characters are then chosen by the class. The teacher should not insist on a "star" performance and should give most

of the pupils the opportunity to participate at one time or another in the dramatization.

41. Have children draw or color pictures describing parts or scenes in the book which they like best, writing beneath the pictures the appropriate sentences or phrases. Have them find and tell the class what phrase or sentence they chose as a basis for their picture.

42. Have pupils work out questions and answers on the lesson in the textbook.

43. In preparation for the textbook lesson have a list of key-words or expressions on the board. Encourage and guide your pupils to build up the textbook selection on the basis of those key-words and expressions, where the content is more or less familiar, as in the case of Bible selections. Where the content of the reading material is unfamiliar let them build up an imaginary story. There is great fun in this exercise and much learning may result.

44. Have a list of key-words on the board, arranged in a random order. Call on pupils to read, in turn, a paragraph or group of sentences from the text, omitting the key-words. Pupils should be asked to fill in the missing words, by referring to the blackboard.

45. Have the pupils study the selection or chapter with the view to recasting a narrative in a dialogue form and vice versa. This exercise may be conducted cooperatively under the teacher's guidance, or each pupil may be asked to work it out independently.

46. Ask pupils to give titles to paragraphs in the selection studied either by choosing expressions from the text or by using original expressions.

47. Have pupils prepare under your guidance an outline or synopsis of the selection read.

48. Have on the board a list of questions of the types, מי עשה? מי אמר? אל מי? מתי? על אדות מי (מה)?. Have pupils answer these by using the textbooks.

49. In longer selections, let the pupils read several paragraphs to themselves. As they finish they raise their hands, and when all have finished, have them give the content in their own words in Hebrew, if it can be done with moderate ease and facility, or else in English.

50. Have pupils select expressions or passages, which appeal to them particularly because of their picturesqueness, forcefulness or poetic imagery.

CHAPTER VII

READING SITUATIONS AND STIMULI

THE SCHOOL AND THE CLASSROOM AS A
PLACE OF LIVING AND EXPERIENCING

Learning has been defined in modern education as the reconstruction of experience. We gain in new insights, in a new sense of values and in new abilities as we come in contact with situations, as we experience their impact upon us, as we undergo the consequence of this experience and learn to evaluate and interpret the consequences. Objects, events, and words gain in meaning in the degree to which our experience with them grows and expands.

Hence, the school and the classroom must provide activities and situations such as are designed to elicit wholehearted desired responses on the part of the pupils and to increase the range and depth of their experiences. What the school, the classroom mean to the pupil depends on the kind of experience he has had with them. The school or the classroom may be either a place of living, of having pleasant relationships and associations; or it may be a place of drudgery and vocabulary grinding. The teacher may be either a source of inspiration, stimulation, and guidance; or a "school-marm," an "old-maid" and a crab.

Children are naturally attentive and curious. Their keen sense of observation and ubiquitous curiosity are proverbial. Novel or unfamiliar things catch their fancy, and they are eager to find out something about them; what they say, what they are for, etc. Here is fertile soil replete with possibilities in the teaching of Hebrew and reading. The classroom, the blackboard and the bulletin board should blaze with stimuli for reading. Written instead of auditory symbols should be employed, whenever possible, provided, of course, these symbols have become sufficiently familiar and intelligible to the children. The pupils should be made to feel that these written groups of words have an important message for them; that they say something they wish, or have, to hear; that they contain something that piques their curiosity. Reading stimuli must, however, be changed around frequently, or they will cease to arouse attention and to elicit a response. There is also the danger that the children may come to associate the meaning with the location rather than with the verbal form of the symbol. Children may delude the teacher into believing that they read meaningful words, while in reality they merely pronounce from memory groups of sounds that they have learned to connect with the particular location on the board, or in the book.

Suggestions for Providing and Utilizing Reading Situations in the Classroom

Following are some suggestions on the utilization of the classroom environment for the enrichment of experiences in relation to reading.

1. Put recurrent class directions on the blackboard instead of giving them orally. Labels and flash cards may be used for this purpose. It will be necessary at first, to tell them what the directions say and to have them learn to read them. They will, however, learn to recognize them in the course of time. Such directions are: סגור את הדלת, סגרו את הספרים, פתחו את הספרים, שבו ישר etc.

2. Write greetings on the board to the boys and to the girls. Have them find the greeting addressed to them, respectively.

3. Label crayon boxes, skull-caps, pencils, etc. with children's Hebrew names. One or two different children may be appointed each day to distribute the articles by reading the labels.

4. Label objects in the room, such as windows, table, blackboard, bulletin board, etc. Take down the labels after class and have the children replace them the following day.

5. The bulletin board is particularly suited to provide a variety of functional reading experiences. It can be used for displaying pictorial and illustrative materials

relative to the lesson, as well as important announcements dealing with school and class activities. However, in order to achieve the most effective results in the use of the bulletin board the following considerations must be kept in mind.

a. The material displayed should be attractively arranged, well-spaced, appropriately mounted, readable. A crowded bulletin board merely confuses the child's mind and fails to attract his attention.

b. Label each picture with a sentence or sentences telling something about it and its place in the story. These labels may be removed at the end of the session, to be replaced appropriately the next day by the pupils.

c. The bulletin board should be dynamic and up to date. The announcements and materials should convey an impression of timeliness. Material which the children have left behind should be discarded. Changes in interest and in materials studied, as well as turns in events of concern to the class, should all be reflected in the displays and items on the bulletin board.

d. The teacher should endeavor to cultivate in the children an interest in the bulletin board and to train them in the habit of watching it for important announcements. These announcements should, of course, be made in simple intelligible Hebrew. Announce each day the Hebrew date; its place in the Jewish calendar; events of interest to the children in the classroom, in the school, in the community, and in the world; approaching holidays; celebrations, etc.

e. Children should be trained to assume gradually and increasingly the responsibility for taking charge of the bulletin board and for keeping it in proper condition. They should also be encouraged to watch for items of interest to be posted, as well as to prepare appropriate drawings and pictures to be mounted.

f. Plan an exhibit of the work of the pupils for parents and visitors. The pupils should take an active part in the planning and in the choosing of the materials to be displayed. The period of planning and preparation of the exhibit should be long enough to allow for adequate learning and practice with the incentive of the exhibit as the desired goal. But due regard must be had for the interest span of the children. If the exhibit is put off too far ahead, it may lose its motive power, and the interest of the children will begin to flag.

6. Outstanding current activities in the community and in the school should, as far as possible, be presented graphically by means of posters and other illustrative materials. An Allied Jewish Appeal Drive,[1] a Jewish National Fund Campaign, Jewish Book Week, or Hebrew Week, etc., should be utilized for Hebrew reading purposes. Hebrew labels comprising appro-

---

[1] This communal activity is designated in different Jewish communities by different names, such as Combined Jewish Drive, Jewish Community Chest, etc.

priate mottos and statements can be prepared and attached to the professional posters issued by the respective organizations, or the class may prepare original Hebrew posters for the particular occasion.

7. Have children keep a scrapbook, where they collect and keep pictures related to their daily lessons. One or more sentences should accompany each of these pictures telling what it is all about. From time to time the children may compare their scrapbooks and, in this manner, review their work.

8. Have a class library. It is desirable to have in each classroom a library center or corner, where books and reading materials suitable to the particular level of the grade should be on display. Picture books, story books, poems, magazines, etc., should be accessible to the children. Responsibility for a well-kept library should be progressively developed in the children. Such a library should include the following available reading materials in Hebrew:

First Level

א) ספרות שינברג – א. י. אייגוס ודניאל פרסקי
ב) מוסף קריאת ענג – ז. חומסקי
ג) ספריה לילדים – ש. מראה־נוף וב. ברודצקי
ד) ספורים יפים[2] – ח. א. פרידלנד
ה) מעשיות לתינוקות, ח"א – צבי שרפשטין

[2] The gradation of these stories in terms of vocabulary difficulties is indicated in the Catalogue of Publications, published by the Bureau of Jewish Education, Cleveland, O.

Second Level

א) ספורים קלים – א. הורוויץ
ב) ספריה לנער, ח"א – ב. רוזן וז. חומסקי
ג) ספורים יפים[2] – ח. א. פרידלנד
ד) אנחנו נוסעים לארץ ישראל – ש. רובינשטין
ה) קריאה להנאה, ח"א – ש. רובינשטין
ו) אוצרי, ח"א – צבי שרפשטין
ז) מעשיות לתינוקות ח"ב – צבי שרפשטין
ח) מקרא ענג – צבי שרפשטין

Third Level

א) ספריה לנער, ח"ב – זאב חומסקי
ב) חנינו ומועדינו – זאב חומסקי
ג) ספורים קצרים – יוסף לבנזון
ד) העם וגבוריו – ש. מראה נוף ויוסף לבנזון
ה) קריאה להנאה, ח"ב – ש. רובינשטין

Fourth Level

א) דוד'ל – ח. א. פרידלנד
ב) ספורי נעם – נ. קרימר
ג) אמנים עברים – צ. שרפשטין
ד) ספר הצחוק – צ. שרפשטין

It should be stated that the term "level" is used here rather loosely and that the division into levels is rather arbitrary. Since there is no general agreement among teachers and authors of children's Hebrew readers with regard to grade placement of vocabularies, it is impossible to determine exactly the level of any particular reading selection or book. Whether a certain selection belongs to one level or to another depends on the series of textbooks used by the respective pupils, rather than on the type or load of vocabulary. When an understanding can be reached in regard to gradation of vocabularies, it will be possible to prepare and grade reading selections objectively and accurately. Until such time reading levels can be set up only approximately and intuitively.

It is advisable to set aside part of the classroom period, regularly, for independent reading. The children should be allowed to choose their reading materials, with the assistance and guidance of the teacher. Each pupil will read as much as he can during this period. Some may finish one story, others more. The teacher must, of course, be on guard to stimulate, prod and direct. Dawdling and woolgathering should be guarded against and discouraged. A chart should be kept, where each pupil will mark down beside his name the books he has finished and the number of pages each of these books contains.

Simple checks on reading should be used, such as are stated above (p. 99). The children may be asked to answer in writing, after completing a story, easy questions such as the following: Did you like the story? Why? What characters did you like in particular?

Who is the hero in the story? Who are the other characters?[3]

Children should be encouraged to take stories out of the library to read outside of class or at home. Special incentives may be offered, but no pressure should be employed. They should be allowed to browse among the books and pamphlets.

All these devices will in the long run result in a much greater interest and facility in reading and in a more rapid growth of vocabulary-comprehension than the intensive study of one or two "basic" textbooks each year.

QUESTIONS AND EXERCISES

Chapters V, VI and VII

1. What are the essential requisites of textbooks in primary Hebrew?

2. How can the lessons in primary Hebrew be made interesting?

3. What do recent studies reveal in regard to the reading interests of children?

---

[3] See an experiment in independent reading reported by Dr. A. Eisenberg in חינוך, edited by Zevi Scharfstein, II, 3.

4. What bearing do the results of these studies have on the problem of preparing textbook and reading materials for the pupils in our elementary grades?

5. What are the stages in the process of learning a language with a reading objective?

6. What is the ultimate objective in this process of language learning? To what extent is this objective attained? How can the situation be remedied?

7. What is meant by a proper reading attitude? What are the weaknesses of oral reading?

8. Suggest some of the devices and methods which may be employed in cultivating a proper reading attitude in the primary grades, also in the more advanced grades.

9. What is the function of flash-cards? List some specific activities where they could be used most effectively.

10. Discuss the place and value of games in the teaching of Hebrew. What are the dangers to be guarded against? How can they be made most profitable?

11. How can the classroom environment be utilized for purposes of stimulating reading activities?

12. How can the bulletin board be made dynamic and functional?

REFERENCES

Brooks, F. D. — *The Applied Psychology of Reading*, Appleton pp. 131–167, also Chapters XIII and XIV.

Buswell, G. T. — *Fundamental Reading Habits*, University of Chicago Press, pp. 58–105.

Cole, R. D.-Tharp, J. B. — *Modern Foreign Languages and Their Teaching*, Appleton-Century, 1937, Chapter V.

Dolch, E. W. — *The Psychology and Teaching of Reading*, Ginn, 1931, Chapters VIII, IX.

Handschin, C. H. — *Modern Language Teaching*, World Book Co., Chapter VIII.

Gates, A. I. — *Interest and Ability in Reading*, Macmillan, Chapters II–IV.

Gray, W. S. — *Summary of Investigations Relating to Reading*, University of Chicago Press, 1925, pp. 9–27, 88–121, 148–190

Judd, C. H and Buswell, G. T. — *Silent Reading*, University of Chicago Press.

Judd, C. H. — *Reading: Its Nature and Development*, University of Chicago Press, pp. 1–14.

Klapper, P. — *Teaching Children to Read*, Appleton, Chapter VIII.

O'Brien, J. A. — *Reading: Its Psychology and Pedagogy*, Century, Chapter X.

Scharfstein, Zevi — דרכי למוד לשוננו, שילה, Chapters XIV, XV.

Smith, Nila B. — *One Hundred Ways of Teaching Silent Reading*, World Book Co., 1925.

Smith, W. A. — *The Reading Process*, Macmillan, pp. 198–225.

Uhl, W. L. — *The Materials of Reading*, Silver-Burdett, Chapters VI, X.

Witty, P. and Kopel, D. — *Reading and the Educative Process*, Ginn, 1939, Chapter II.

Chapter VIII

THE USE OF PHONETICS IN TEACHING READING IN THE PRIMARY GRADES

General Considerations

Although the ability to recognize word-wholes and thought-units is the ultimate objective in the teaching of reading in the primary grades, this ability can be achieved only as a result of adequate training and experience. The young and immature reader is not readily equal to this task. Words which are distinctive in size, shape, or component elements will be learned and recognized with comparative ease. But words possessing common features will be mistaken for one another. For example, words like יודע, עומד, מדוע; or like שמע, שמה, משה, and so on, must be carefully studied and analyzed into their constituent elements. Unless the pupil is trained to recognize individual characteristics and striking elements of the word, he will be at a loss for clues to unravel new or unfamiliar reading matter.

Attention must be focused on the role of these elements as parts of the whole and not as isolated units; just as a cog of a wheel is recognized as such when viewed in its relation to the whole, that is as a part of the total pattern scheme and not as an isolated piece of iron. In other words, to react to the letter שׁ as a part of the word שׁמשׁ is not the same as to react to this letter in isolation. This distinction must be borne in mind in the teaching procedure, and transfer must be made frequently from the complete word to the individual element and back again to the total word.

For purposes of illustration, let us take the analogy from making acquaintance with people. The first time the person is introduced, whose name is known to us (= a word that has meaning for us in its auditory form), a certain general impression, or an outstanding characteristic is left with us, which may or may not be sufficient to identify the same person when met in a different group or environment. The more conspicuous the individual characteristics, the greater the likelihood of recognizing this new acquaintance. Lacking adequate distinguishing characters, we may recognize this acquaintance in the same house, with the same group of friends, and in the same environment. But we are likely to be in an embarrassing predicament when called upon to identify him in a new environment amongst strangers, especially in the company of his twin brother or of somebody else who resembles him. A further study of details and closer familiarity are necessary in order to make recognition more certain and definite. After meeting the two acquaintances often enough, and after building up sufficiently clear total impressions of them, certain typical and peculiar characteristics become dominant and serve as *subconscious* clues, by which we are able to identify them respectively at a glance. In sum, these two principles operate in the process of identifying persons as well as in that of recognizing words: (1) *bring details into consciousness* and (2) *by practice render them unconscious again.*

The technique outlined here is based on the analytic-synthetic method in teaching reading. Children first learn to recognize brief outlines and thought-units. They are then trained to master the reading of the words composing these sentences or thought-units. Eventually, they are guided to analyze out, gradually and systematically, certain sounds comprising the words mastered. Finally, these compound sounds are recombined into words and thought-units. This process of focusing attention on the individual sounds and component elements of the words is called *phonetic training.*

The need for phonetic training differs with the individual pupil. Some children will be seriously handicapped in their reading progress, unless a considerable amount of phonetic training is provided for them. Others need a moderate amount of such training, while still others will learn to read without any phonetic training whatsoever. However, very few people, children or adults, are found to be reading at their own maximum rates even in their native tongue. Techniques and procedures for the improvement of the reading rates, without loss in comprehension, such as speed drills and short exposure exercises, can and should be employed with varying degrees of frequency for the poor as well as for the better readers.

Since there are very rare occasions for the pupils of the primary grades to read or use script writing, there seems to be no justification for any emphasis on writing or for the use of script writing in these grades. Manuscript or print-script writing should be used exclusively in these grades. It is more legible, it is easier to master, it can be correlated with the printed forms used in reading and thus serves as an aid to reading; and the difficulty of introducing two sets of symbols simultaneously is thereby avoided. Experimentations and studies have demonstrated beyond a doubt that the learning of reading is facilitated by the use of manuscript writing. According to an English investigator[1] many problems over which ophthalmologists have worked for years were eliminated by manuscript writing. The transition from this type of writing to script is very simple and easy in the more

[1] E. Gill, quoted by Agnes de Lima, *The Little Red School House*, Macmillan, 1942, p. 140.

advanced grades, especially if the relationship in form between these two types of the alphabet is pointed out. According to a recent survey, the prevailing practice in the American schools is to use the manuscript writing in the first two grades.[2]

How Children Learn to Recognize Words

Students of methods employed by children at the initial stages of learning to read, in attacking and mastering words, reveal several types of observation. On the basis of these studies a variety of techniques may be suggested which will be helpful in training children to recognize new words. They are as follows:

1. *Perception of Minor Distinctive Features* — Such differences may be of little intrinsic value, but will be a useful aid in identification, such as the "long neck" of the ל in שלום, or the "little head" of the *Yod* in בית, the "two eyes and nose" in the vowels of שמש.

2. *Difference in Size or Color* — The general conclusion of experimenters is "That whatever serves to distinguish a thing from a group makes it better remembered."[3] Peterson[4] found that for immediate recall of a series, variations in size offered a slight advantage,

---

[2] See Frank N. Freeman — "A Survey of Manuscript Writing in the Public Schools," Elementary School Journal XLVI (March 1946), 375-80

[3] H. R. Huse, *Psychology of Foreign Language Study*, Chapel Hill, University of North Carolina, 1931, p. 53.

[4] Quoted *ibidem*.

that of color was of no aid, and variation in the style of the print was detrimental. However, in recall after 24 hours, the result was quite different. Size was the best variation, color next, while even form (print) variations showed a gain of 19 per cent. In presenting vocabulary on the blackboard or in mimeographed reading matter, this device of differentiation can be used extensively.

3. *Varying the Relative Position of the Word in the Phrase or Sentence* — Children generally recognize a word by its special location on the page or blackboard or by a certain sequence in the phrase or sentence. But they may fail to identify the same word in a different location or word-order. Hence care must be taken to introduce the particular word in varying locations on the board or reading matter, and in a variety of situations of word sequence. The word ספר, for example, will be more readily differentiated after seeing it in such a variety of sentences as הילד קורא בספר, קח את הספר וקרא, הספר על השלחן.

4. *Phonetic Study and Analysis* — Certain letters of the word should be studied and analyzed out by underlining or encircling them, also by noting the respective sequence of the letters in the word, such as the difference in the order of the ש and the מ in the words עמש, משה, and שמש. Certain letter combinations and blends which are of high frequency should be studied as units, without analysis of components, as, for example, the

USE OF PHONETICS 137

phonograms ‎נוּ–, ‎נִ–, ‎ים–, ‎וּת–, etc. However, such phonetic analysis should be carried on in a moderate degree. Too much attention to phonetic detail leads to letter consciousness and phonogram juggling. Pupils may develop the mechanical or "sound" approach, instead of the "meaning" approach, to the reading materials. Constant emphasis should be placed on the letter or vowel as a component of the total word, which, in turn, represents meaning and is part of a larger sense-pattern; and the transfer from the phonetic analysis to the perception of the total configuration of word and context should be made as frequently as possible.

5. *Syllabification* — The unit of pronunciation is the syllable, not the letter. The letter and, in the case of Hebrew, also the vowel, have no independent functional existence. In practice they are employed only in combination. They should, therefore, not be studied in isolation. Only after seeing the letter in combination with different vowels, and after encountering the vowel in combination with the different letters, should the respective phonetic characters be abstracted and identified. Thus, the word should first be broken up into parts or syllables, and then, after studying the syllables, in which a certain letter recurs with a variety of vowels, or vice versa, the sound of the letter, or of the vowel, as the case may be, should be emphasized. At no time, however, should the syllable, or the individual sound,

be treated otherwise than as an integral part of the word-whole or thought-unit.

6. *Analytical Examination* — Children should be trained to recognize the total word by identifying mentally or visually the component parts of the word. This procedure is to be distinguished from *analytical pronunciation*, in which these sounds or letters are sounded out separately before the total word is recognized. Thus, in seeing a word, the child may receive the stimulation from the several consonants and vowels of which the word is composed, but the final reaction is that of reading the word as a whole and not that of deciphering it sound-by-sound. The child may "see" the sounds, but he need not translate them into the sound equivalents, just as he may recognize a picture by examining the component details and features, but without thinking of them in terms of sound equivalents. At the initial stages some measure of lip-movement may be noted, but this will gradually disappear as a result of training in the habit of focusing attention on the word-whole. The recognition of a word as a composite of integral parts should no more depend on the need of sounding the parts separately than the recognition of a picture should necessitate naming the detailed features by which it is identified. Analytical pronunciation should be avoided, but analytical examination should be encouraged. Children should be trained, in encountering unfamiliar words, to examine

and study them silently, that is, to "think" the words before they read them as wholes. Choppy reading by sounding letters one by one should be discouraged.

7. *Inference From Context* — A moderate measure of "guessing" the word by its context is wholesome and should not be discountenanced. Success in language learning is largely dependent on this type of guessing or inference. This practice places the emphasis where it should be, namely, on looking for meaning. There is, of course, the danger of wrong guessing, against which teachers must guard. But the dependence on context provides excellent opportunities for gain in power of inference and in the habit of centering attention on content, and these opportunities outweigh the possible dangers of "careless" reading. The probability of wrong guessing is, of course, in direct proportion to the density of new or unfamiliar words. Where these words are spread very thinly in the reading material, the chance of wrong guessing is reduced to a negligible minimum.

All these devices in attacking new or unfamiliar reading material are helpful, and they can be used, in turn, at one time or another. After the pupils have learned to recognize and to read with some degree of facility some forty or fifty words, composing the lessons studied during the first couple of months and after they have acquired more or less the attitude of looking

140 HOW TO TEACH ELEMENTARY HEBREW

for meaning in the reading matter, a systematic effort should be made to inculcate these various methods of observation and analysis.

Specific Steps in the Process of Learning to Read

Specifically, the process of learning to read a new language consists of the following successive stages:

I. Building up mental auditory reactions to a limited number of new words and expressions, so that whenever they are presented orally an ideational response spontaneously follows; that is, the idea or meaning flashes through the mind immediately upon hearing them.

II. Acquiring the ability of recognizing the visual representations, or "pictures," of the words and expressions, which were learned orally. These words are to be mastered first as sight-words, that is, as words that can be identified instantly as thought-content, without being conscious of the component individual sounds. For example, the child should learn to read with understanding words and expressions like סֵפֶר; הַיֶּלֶד הוֹלֵךְ; etc., without being aware of, or able to read, the individual sounds composing these words.

III. Developing a technique of analysis and synthesis, which will facilitate the attack on, and recognition of, newly presented reading material. For this purpose, a program of phonetic training and phonic exercises must be carefully planned and put into practice. In planning such a program the following considerations must be borne in mind:

1. Phonic exercises are an aid to reading; but they should not be confused with reading and the reading lesson, where the emphasis is on comprehension. Hence, phonic exercises should be conducted at a period set aside for this purpose.

2. Before children have acquired the technique of attacking new words successfully they should not be asked to read meaningful material, which is not within their oral vocabulary, since the words convey no meaning to them, and they have, therefore, no means of checking the results of their efforts. In presenting new words as reading material during the early stages, the words should be read and explained by the teacher, before expecting pupils to read them.

3. The mechanics of the word should not receive concentrated attention until the pupils have acquired the *attitude of reading for meaning*, or until they have learned a considerable number of sight-words and can note points of similarity or difference in these words.

4. Phonetic instructions should be given in moderation and in accordance with the particular needs of the pupils. Over-emphasis of phonics develops phonic jugglers, whose attention is focused on sounds rather than on meaning. Subdividing the class into groups,

whenever possible, for the purpose of phonetic instruction, is highly advisable.

5. The procedure in phonetic instruction should be from the complex to the simple and back to the complex. The sentence, phrase or word should be analyzed, and the particular phonic element, or elements, under consideration, should be isolated and stressed within the natural setting — the word or sentence. But the skill learned in isolation should be immediately applied and practised in context reading.

6. Phonetic training should be functional, that is, only those elements should be stressed in a particular period, which recur most frequently in the corresponding reading lesson. Furthermore, as previously stated, no isolated elements should be practiced except in their natural setting, namely, in the word; and only in such words as the pupil has encountered, or is likely to encounter in the immediate future.

7. Preparatory to *visual discrimination of sounds*, a certain amount of training in *auditory discrimination* should be given. Various games and devices involving the recognition of sounds in auditory situations are suggested below.

8. Right-to-left reading habits should not be taken for granted. They should be systematically trained and practiced by special techniques, such as chart-building, oral reading and emphasizing initial sounds, also by moving pointer or finger from right to left

beneath each word, sentence or line. These sweeps of the pointer or finger should be manipulated systematically, leading from emphasis on word, to sweeps including several words, a sentence, and finally to sweeps along the whole line.

9. No single device or game should be overworked. Repeated passive acceptance of a certain game by the pupils should not be mistaken for active interest.

Devices and Games

The following is a selected list of devices and games which may be used as aids in phonic instruction:

1. Have children identify a particular sound at the beginning, in the middle, or at the end of the word, as the case may be, by reciting a list of words known to the children and having them raise their hands when the word containing this sound is heard. For example: Have them identify the שׁ at the beginning of such words as שָׁמַע, שָׁמַיִם, שָׁם, etc.; or in the middle of the words משה, ישב, etc.; or at the end of the words ראש, שמש, שלש, etc.

2. Let the teacher, followed by pupils in turn, whisper certain words, which the pupils should be asked to recognize by watching the movements of the lips and tongue.

3. Have children identify words that rhyme in poems or song.

4. Mention a word, then have children in turn mention words, beginning with the final letter of the word mentioned by the preceding person, thus: דבר, ילד; משה, שלום; שמש, ראש; etc.

5. Have pupils keep an alphabetic dictionary of their own making, and have them enter daily the new words learned or encountered. A sentence or phrase may be added incorporating the new word and illustrating its meaning. Whenever possible, a picture should be introduced to convey the meaning.

6. Pronounce words and ask the children whether a given consonant sound is at the beginning or at the end of the word.

7. List words that can be made into new word-forms by adding or prefixing certain phonic elements, such as ‒ת, ‒ְי, ‒ֵנוּ, ‒ִים, ‒נוּ, ‒ְתָ, ‒ְתִי, etc., e. g., הָלַכְתִּי, תִּשְׁמַע, יִשְׁמַע, בֵּיתֵנוּ, שִׁירִים, עָמַדְנוּ, יָשַׁבְתָּ, etc. However, care should be taken not to introduce word-forms that involve principles with which the children are not familiar. One principle at a time, or confusion will arise.

8. Have pupils underline or encircle similar elements in a given list of words, e.g., דלת, חדר; שלש, שמים; שמש, מורה, etc.

9. Building up familiar words from a given list of syllables. Arrange the syllables in one column and number them. Ask the pupils to give you the numbers which make up certain familiar words which you have

given them either orally or in writing. For example, the parts 1) יָ, 2) ית, 3) דָר, 4) לת, 5) לְד, 6) בַּ, 7) ח, 8) דְ, will yield the words דֶּלֶת, חֶדֶר, בַּיִת, יֶלֶד.

10. Have children find smaller words within big ones by underlining or encircling the smaller parts, e.g., הַתַּלְמִידִים, שָׁמַיִם, בָּרֹאשׁ, בֵּית־הַסֵּפֶר, טוֹבָה, שִׁירִים, etc.

11. Give pupils a word or a group of consonants and have them build up, with the component consonants, as many words as they can think of. For example, the word שמים contains the consonants of such words as שָׁם, מַיִם, מִי, שְׁמִי, מִי שָׁם, שֵׁם, יֵשׁ, etc.; with the consonants of אָכַלְתִּי can be built up such words as אֵת, אַתְּ, אָכַל, לִי, לֹא, כָּל, אֵל, etc.

12. Have on the blackboard a chart of common phonic characteristics (phonograms, letters, or vowels) and have the words classified into "families." The families may be composed of the following categories: (a) words beginning with the same phonogram, e.g., יוֹשֵׁב, יוֹצֵא, יוֹדֵעַ, etc.; (b) words ending in the same phonogram, e.g. הוֹלְכִים, יְלָדִים, סְפָרִים; שָׁב, יוֹשֵׁב, כּוֹתֵב, etc.; (c) words beginning with the same letter, e.g., בֵּית־הַסֵּפֶר, בַּיִת, בּוּכֶה; אוֹמֵר, אַתָּה, אֲנִי; (d) words ending in the same letter, e.g., שֵׁם, שָׁלוֹם; or שְׂמָךְ, הוֹלֵךְ, אֵיךְ; (e) words comprising the same letter, e.g., חָכָם, אֶחָד, צוֹחֵק; and (f) words comprising the same vowel-sign, e.g., שֵׁם, צוֹחֵק, יוֹשֵׁב. Ask the children to classify the words they have learned in accordance with the respective "families" or categories.

13. Have a double set of word-cards distributed among the pupils. Call upon two children with words unalike and ask them to pass around the room in search of the duplicates of their respective cards. As the child passes each desk he must read each child's card. The owner of the card is responsible for the correctness of the reading. The one that finds his partner first, wins.

14. Pronounce to the pupils words containing certain common elements. Have the children listen for, and identify, these common elements.

15. Have children recall, or find, words containing the phonic elements newly learned.

16. Keep on the blackboard or bulletin board a cumulative or progressive chart indicating and adding each day the letters thus far learned. The chart may bear the title: We have learned the following letters: . . .

17. Refer to the subsequent chapter for dictionary activities. See also above, Chapter VI, for further suggestions of games and activities.

QUESTIONS AND EXERCISES

1. What is meant by phonetic training? What place should it occupy in the reading program? Why is it needed? When?

2. How does phonetic training in the analytic-

synthetic method differ from the synthetic or phonic method in the teaching of reading?

3. Should the script writing be taught to children in the early grades? Why?

4. What are the various techniques which children are found to employ in attacking and mastering words in reading? What conclusions can we draw from these findings as to phonetic training?

5. Distinguish between analytical examination and analytical pronunciation.

6. What are the specific stages in learning to read a new language?

7. What devices should be used to guard the pupils against becoming letter-conscious or sound-conscious?

REFERENCES

Brooks, F. D. — *The Applied Psychology of Reading*, Appleton, pp. 168–238.
Buswell, G. T. — *Fundamental Reading Habits*, University of Chicago Press, pp. 106–148.
Dolch, E. W. — *Teaching Primary Reading*, Garard Press, Chapter XI.
Gates, A. I. — *New Methods in Primary Reading*, Teachers College, Columbia University, Chapter IV.
———, *Interest and Ability in Reading*, Macmillan, Chapter VII.
Judd, C. H. — *Reading· Its Nature and Development*, pp. 6–8, 128, 135–141.
Klapper, P. — *Teaching Children to Read*, Appleton, Chapter IX.
O'Brien, J. A — *Reading: Its Psychology and Pedagogy*, Century, Chapter IX
Smith, W. A. — *The Reading Process*, Macmillan, pp. 88–106.
Twenty-fourth Yearbook of the National Society for the Study of Education, Part I, pp. 81–91.

Chapter IX

VOCABULARY STUDIES AS A BASIS FOR THE READING PROGRAM

In undertaking any project or program the determination of the aim is essential to its success. A clear perspective of the objectives and a systematic organization of steps calculated to lead to the achievement of these objectives, make for economy in effort and in time and for definite progress.

The Word List Trend

During the past two decades it has become increasingly clear to students of linguistic pedagogy that, in the final analysis, learning a language is largely a matter of learning specific vocabularies. One does not learn a language in general, but rather certain words and expressions for which a need arises or is created. Some words are more serviceable than others, depending upon the need or purpose, and should, therefore, be given priority in the pedagogic program. Hence, word-counts and the construction of word lists have become the order of the day in programs of language instruction, whether native or foreign. Courses of study in language are based on standardized word lists, and publishers insist that authors of children's literature and of textbooks in language operate with such word lists.

As was indicated in a preceding chapter, there are generally four major language abilities: speaking, listening, writing and reading. Each of these abilities involves a specific vocabulary and a distinct methodology. Furthermore, vocabularies differ, even within the same ability, in accordance with the differences of social caste, or of vocational groups.

Consequently, workers in the field have been busily engaged in investigations and in searching for criteria for the selection and standardization of word lists. In 1921 Thorndike published *The Teacher's Word Book*, a reading word list in English, consisting of 10,000 words occurring most frequently in English reading materials. Numerous investigations have since been carried on to determine minimum essential vocabularies on the basis of frequency in reading, as well as in writing and speaking, both in English and in foreign languages.

Word-counts in Hebrew

Very little research along these lines has been done in Hebrew. But even as far back as 1882, William R. Harper, then professor of Hebrew and Cognate Languages, Chicago Baptist Union Theological Seminary, reputed to have been a teacher endowed with unusual pedagogic intuition, conceived the idea of counting and tabulating the vocabulary occurring with a high degree of frequency in the Hebrew Bible (25–5,000 times), in order to facilitate the study of this Book. He compiled lists of words which include the following categories: I. Verbs occurring 500–5,000 times, II. Verbs occurring 200–500 times, III. Verbs occurring 100–200 times, IV. Verbs occurring 50–100 times, V. Verbs occurring 25–50 times, VI. Nouns occurring 500–5,000 times, VII. Nouns occurring 300–500 times, VIII. Nouns occurring 200–300 times, IX. Nouns occurring 100–200 times, X. Nouns occurring 50–100 times, XI. Nouns occurring 25–50 times.

In his introduction to these word lists, Harper makes the following significant observation: "Out of the seven or eight thousand vocables in the Hebrew language, about *one thousand* occur over twenty-five times. If the learner will commit five or six of these a day, within six or eight months he will have mastered a vocabulary sufficient to enable him to read any portion of the Hebrew of the Old Testament with ease and pleasure. Three words, those meaning *to say*, *God*, and *son*, occupy sixty pages of the Hebrew text. The sixty verbs given in Lists I and II (occurring 200–5,000 times) occupy *two hundred* pages, and the first sixty nouns given in Lists VI and VII (occurring 300–5,000 times) occupy *two hundred and twenty-five pages* —

together about one-third of the whole Bible, and in this derivatives are not included."[1]

It should be pointed out that a *word* in Harper's list is a rootword, although he also gives, in the case of verbs, the conjugation variants and the frequency of their respective recurrence. It may also be noted that despite the painstaking care with which this great scholar worked, some errors have crept into his lists. This is, of course, understandable and pardonable, in view of the magnitude of the task, which he had to perform all by himself, with assistance only from his brother. The wonder is that the errors are so few.

Studies of Minimum Essentials in Language

Various studies conducted more recently in modern European languages, as well as in Hebrew, serve to confirm Harper's observation in regard to the limited number of words actually needed not only in the case of the Bible, but also in that of modern literary texts. The same is true with respect to the extent of the vocabulary needed for purposes of speech and writing, whether in Hebrew or in any other language. For example, according to Michael West, a thousand-word vocabulary in English, which a foreign child of

[1] William R. Harper, *Hebrew Vocabularies*, Chicago, 1882.

average intelligence can learn in about three years, is capable of telling in easy and effective style a 50,000-word novel, constituting a book of about 150 pages in the usual format. Any full-length English novel may be rewritten, according to him, in about 2,000 basic words, without tampering to any marked degree with either the content or the style of the author, although from 5,000 to 7,000 words are needed for reading easily unaltered versions of those commonly read.[2]

Similarly, the author of *The System of Basic English*, 1934, C. K. Ogden, has demonstrated that 850 basic words will serve all purposes of clear and adequate expression in English. As an illustration, he reproduced an address by Franklin Delano Roosevelt, letters by famous personalities and articles in leading magazines, all within the framework of these 850 basic words, without loss in clarity.

Ogden's word list is based on utility rather than frequency. Instead of choosing words of highest frequency, he endeavored to discover which are the most essential ideas we wish to express and what words will express these ideas most economically. The number 850 was chosen rather arbitrarily; (a) because it represents the number of words that can "legibly be printed on the back of a single sheet of note paper," and (b) because this number of words can be mem-

[2] Cf. Michael West, *Language in Education*, Longmans, Green, 1932, Chapter V.

orized in a comparatively short time and is sufficient to express all meaning essential to normal, non-technical discourse.

Ogden's approach, although very ingenious, suffers from oversimplification and rationality. There is too much emphasis in this approach on language as a synthesis of words with specific meanings and too little regard for the irrational aspect of language. Indeed, in teaching a language with a reading objective we are particularly interested in this irrational aspect, in idioms and locutions, in which words are combined, with modifications of their simple meaning. It is this aspect which gives language its distinctive traditional character. Our chief objective is, after all, to have our pupils find their way progressively into literary materials, where the traditional, figurative and idiomatic elements of the language predominate. Hence, for our purposes, occurrence frequency in reading materials, rather than utility and simplicity will have to serve as our criterion for selection of vocabulary.

A fairly extensive investigation of Hebrew vocabularies was published by Eliezer Rieger.[3] With the assistance of a group of teachers and principals in Palestine, Rieger examined 200,000 running words, which he classified in terms of occurrence-frequency. These words were obtained as follows: (a) One third

[3] אליעזר ריגר, אוצר מלות היסוד, הוצאת בית המדרש למורים עברים, ירושלים, תרצ"ה.

from private letters and free compositions by 286 pupils; (b) one third from private and business letters of 521 adults, city dwellers as well as villagers; (c) one third from classical sources, such as the narrative portions of the Bible, as well as typical selections from the *Mishnah*, *Aggadah* and the Prayer Book. The sum total of the basic words examined, excepting repetitions and basic word-forms, amounted to 5,892. But only 2,017 words of the total occur ten times and over in the materials examined, and these were included in the basic word list.

Rieger, accordingly, reaches the conclusion that only 2,000 selected basic words may be said to constitute the essence or body of the language, since these represent 95 per cent of the running words in the materials investigated. The thousands of other words found in these materials are of such infrequent usage as to be ignored, since they form only 5 per cent of the total running words. Of these 2,000 words, arranged in the order of occurrence-frequency, the first hundred represent 41 per cent, the first five hundred — 72 per cent, and the first thousand — 85 per cent of the total running words. Consequently, a person who has learned the first 500 words has mastered 72 per cent of the language needed for reading and writing usage.

A vocabulary analysis of the individual books of the Hebrew Bible, made under the supervision of the writer, points to similar conclusions. For example, the abridged book of *Bereshit* (in Scharfstein's edition) comprises 1,069 words,[4] of which 411 occur only once and only 332 occur with a frequency of five and above. But these 332 words constitute 88 per cent of the running words in the book and are, with few exceptions, words of high frequency (25–5,000 times) in the entire Bible. The case of *Bereshit* is typical of the other narrative books of the Bible.

The Need of Basic Word Lists in Hebrew

In the light of all this it seems quite clear that if our major objective in the teaching of Hebrew in the primary grades is, as we claim, to prepare our pupils for the study of the Bible, a mastery of some 400 essential words should be adequate for this purpose. Such a task is not beyond the reach of the average primary pupil, in the course of about two years. In fact, the majority of our Hebrew textbooks in vogue in our primary grades, even the first-year readers, operate with a vocabulary of over 400 words. Yet, the results fall far short of our purpose. Our pupils are not prepared, even at the end of two years, for an intelligent and appreciative study of the Bible.

[4] A word in this instance is defined as a noun in all its inflections, singular or plural, and a verb in all tenses in the same conjugation. Where the difference in number — in the case of nouns — and in tense — in the case of verbs — yields a radically changed form, it is regarded as a new word. Since recognition rather than recall is our major aim in the study of Hebrew, this definition of a word may be considered adequate.

The reasons are not far to seek. In the first place, our textbooks, in the main, even those pretending to prepare the pupils specifically for the Bible, fail to incorporate a significant proportion of the essential biblical words. An analysis of these textbooks reveals that only about 50% of their respective vocabularies are of high biblical frequency (25–5,000 times). The choice of vocabulary seems to be largely a matter of subjective judgment and experience of the authors. In the second place, the vocabulary load in these textbooks is far too heavy for thorough mastery.

Mere intuition and opinion, even those of experts and experienced teachers, have been proven to be utterly inadequate as a basis for selection of vocabulary. One need only examine the wide divergence in the vocabulary range of elementary textbooks in Hebrew and the arbitrariness with which "easy" and "difficult" words are determined in children's Hebrew literature and magazines, such as the *Ha-Do'ar La-No'ar*, to be convinced of the unreliability of expert opinion in this regard. Rieger concludes after comparing the views of a group of eight experts in the field, including veteran teachers, authors of children's readers and an editor of children's periodicals, on a sampling of objectively selected words, as follows: "... it is impossible to rely in this respect on the experience and opinions of expert pedagogues, let alone the experience and opinions of teachers in general. The only reliable basis for the organization of a course of study of this type is an objective word-count."[5] The same conclusion was reached by other investigators in the field.

Gates maintains, on the basis of his investigations, "That for the average pupil it is desirable to provide materials sufficient to give about forty running words for every new word introduced during the first year. During the first few months, more material per new word is needed than later, but even during the second year, the material should show at least a ratio of thirty-five running words to each new word."[6] The majority of textbooks in English, the investigators complain, provide only fourteen running words to every new word. The ratio in our Hebrew textbooks is about five running words to each new word, and this in a language foreign to the child. Is there any wonder that the grasp, among our children, of their Hebrew vocabulary is so flimsy and that the impressions made by these words is so fleeting?

The solution is, of course, obvious. We must reduce considerably the framework of limited vocabularies and, above all, we must exercise greater care in the choice of our vocabularies, reducing to a minimum the proportion

---

[5] Op. cit , p. 20.
[6] Arthur I. Gates, *The Improvement of Reading*, Revised Edition, Macmillan, 1935, p. 267 f.

of non-essential words. Such words serve little purpose in terms of growth in language power, beyond overtaxing the retentive capacity of the pupils and thereby weakening their grasp of essential words.

In discussing the learning of Hebrew with the view to preparation for the Bible and the other classics of Hebrew literature, it is necessary to consider, to be sure, the question of grammatical constructions, style and idiom, which characterize these books. Our writers of textbooks and children's literature, who shy from all stylistic and grammatical difficulties and avoid idiomatic expressions, preferring to write in a simple, wishy-washy, "childish" style, are shirking their responsibility. In stripping the language of its figurative and idiomatic elements, they commit the same error as does Ogden in his *Basic English* approach. But while Ogden may be justified on the grounds that he is interested in speeding the progress of English toward becoming a world language, our concern is primarily to introduce our pupils as quickly as possible to the literary style, in which our classical writings are encased. The transition from the "simple" Hebrew to the classical style is too abrupt and must, of necessity, leave the pupils handicapped and in a state of mental confusion. On the other hand, a narrow range of a limited vocabulary should make it possible to concentrate greater attention on the grammatical, stylistic and idiomatic peculiarities of classical literature, and to transmit these in a gradual and systematic manner, leading the pupils progressively into the style of the classic books.

Steps in the Reading Program

To sum up, the reading aim in the teaching of Hebrew adopted as basic in the present discussion, implies a program comprising the following steps:

1. The preparation of word lists chosen on the principle of frequency of use and occurrence in the biblical and other literary selections, which the pupils will be expected to read and study in the more advanced grades.

2. Subdivision of these lists for purposes of grade-placement in accordance with their respective rank in the frequency lists and with the mental and experiential maturity of the pupils.

3. The adoption of textbooks and reading materials for each grade in terms of the degree of correlation of their respective vocabularies with the word lists for the particular grade.

4. The adaptation and creation of materials, for extensive reading as well as for intensive study, within the restricted vocabularies for each grade and providing for a high degree of recurrence frequency of these vocabularies. In the preparation of these materials,

it is, of course, necessary to take into account the background and the potential interests of the children, as well as the desirability of extending and enriching these interests in behalf of Jewish and human purposes.

5. Systematic and progressive training in independent reading. This implies provision for large amounts of reading matter, designed to develop comprehension in large eyefuls, graded in difficulty, adapted to the tastes of the individual pupils and based on limited vocabularies.

THE ASSOCIATED TALMUD TORAHS WORD LIST

A committee headed by the author, charged with the task of investigating the problems relative to the study of Hebrew in the primary grades, under the auspices of Associated Talmud Torahs of Philadelphia, under the direction of the late Ben Rosen, undertook several years ago to organize a basic vocabulary for the first three years. In preparation for this step a study was made of the vocabularies of *Bereshit* and *Shemot*, the books generally studied in the third and fourth years, as well as of the words that are functional in the classroom, in the Jewish home, in ceremonials, and in the synagogue. The three-year word list was then compiled including the following categories:

1. Words that occur most frequently in the Bible (50–5,000 times).

2. Words that occur ten times or over (but less than 50 times) in the Bible and are of frequent occurrence in *Bereshit* and *Shemot*.
3. Functional words.
4. Words that are common to the seven textbooks, out of the twenty examined and evaluated, selected for the first three years.

The basic vocabulary consisting of 740 words was then subdivided into three groups and arranged for each of the three grades on the basis of their relative rank in the above-mentioned categories and of their being common to the textbooks for the particular year.

In order to establish further the validity of the word list as a preparatory language basis for the study of the Bible and simple narrative Hebrew, the word list was evaluated in terms of the following criteria:[7]

1. Correlation of the word list and general Bible frequency.
2. Correlation of the word list and occurrence-frequency in *Bereshit* and *Shemot*.
3. Correlation of the word list and Rieger's word list (first 500 words "representing 72 per cent of the language").

How to Use the Word List in the Classroom

These word lists are now available in printed form, both in separate parts, with the English translations,

[7] See William Chomsky, "Vocabulary Studies as a Basis for a Hebrew Methodology," *Jewish Education*, IX, 2.

and in consolidated form, alphabetically arranged. They may, accordingly be used as dictionaries. Some of the ways in which these "dictionaries" may be used are as follows:

1. The children locate and check off regularly in their "dictionaries" the newly-learned words.

2. The children compose a parallel and progressive dictionary of their own, in their copybooks. As they learn new words they are asked to enter them in their "dictionaries," using the word list dictionary as a guide. A sentence illustrating the sense or use of the word may be added alongside each word, for the purpose of recall or review.

3. Have the children review periodically the vocabularies they have learned. Give the review words on the blackboard or on a mimeographed sheet and have the children locate these words in their "dictionaries" and get their meanings. Ask them to illustrate these words by means of sentences, either copied from the book, in the case of first-grade children; or original sentences, in the case of more advanced pupils. These exercises may be assigned as homework.

4. Distribute labels or cards with words or sentences on them. Have children arrange the words in alphabetical order, using the "dictionary" as a guide.

5. Write a column of words on the board. Have children arrange these words in an alphabetical order, with the aid of their "dictionaries."

6. Distribute mimeographed lists of review words. Have children arrange them either in the classroom or at home in an alphabetical order.

7. Play a game of identical consonants. One child reads from the dictionary a word beginning with a certain consonant (e. g., בָּנָד). Let this child challenge a child from another team to find another word, without looking in his dictionary, that begins with the same consonant (e. g., בַּיִת) and give its meaning. A definite length of time should, of course, be allowed in each case for the finding of these words.

8. In the grades above the first the children may be asked occasionally to prepare the new lessons with the aid of the dictionary, after the lesson is properly motivated and the curiosity of the pupils is aroused as to what follows. To facilitate this procedure the children may be given a list of the new or "key" words and expressions, the meanings of which they are to find in their "dictionaries," before reading the selection assigned. A list of questions to be answered from the new lesson will serve as an added incentive and check up.

In this way, the children of the primary grades learn in a lifelike and functional manner the proper use of a dictionary and the order of the Hebrew alphabet. They also have their attention focused on the sound of individual letters in a natural situation; namely, where the letter is not an isolated, arbitrary and meaningless unit, but a component element of a meaningful word-whole in a context of meaning.

The Junior Hebrew Library Word List

Another project on which the above-mentioned Committee wished to embark was the preparation of appropriate reading materials within the vocabulary range of the pupils in each grade, beginning with the first. A long-range plan was projected with the view to adapting selections from Hebrew literature and Jewish folklore in terms of the specific vocabularies, and thus make available to our pupils some of the best in our literary creations which have stood the test of time, incidental to the study of essential vocabulary.

This project drew the attention of several educational agencies in a number of Jewish communities in this country, which undertook to collaborate in sponsoring it. A committee representing these agencies was consequently set up, under the chairmanship of the author, to supervise the execution of this Junior Hebrew Library project.

In order to meet the needs of the schools conducted under the auspices of the various bureaus in the country and to gain nation-wide acceptance for the word lists as a basis for the preparation of new text materials and for the projected Junior Hebrew Library, the Committee deemed it necessary to revise the above-mentioned word list. The revised word list, it was felt, should incorporate words of high frequency in the Bible (100 to 5,000) and in Rieger's list (first 500 words), as well as words that are common, in the main, to the textbooks generally in vogue in our schools for the first two years. Eleven popular primary textbooks were analyzed for this purpose. The resultant wordlist, consisting of 370 words, was ultimately approved by the Committee as the basis for the first level of the Junior Hebrew Library.

The reading selections in the first series of *Sifriyah La-Noʻar* were written within the framework of these 370 words. This series included adaptations of stories by J. L. Perez, Sholem Asch, A. Z. Rabinowitz, some folk stories, and an original biography of Theodore Herzl. In the preparation of the second series of the *Sifriyah*, it was deemed advisable to increase the basic word list by about 100 words, comprising such as occur in the Bible 100 times and over and ten times and over in the books of *Bereshit* and *Shemot*, as well as numerals and other highly functional words. This composite word list, constituting a total of 466 words, served as a basis for the second series of *Sifriyah La-Noʻar*, published by the Board of Jewish Education of Baltimore, as well as for the anthology of Jewish holidays and festivals, *Ḥaggenu u-Moʻadenu*, published under the auspices of the Histadruth Ivrith of America. This list should form an adequate framework for the lengthy stories, novelettes, biographies, etc., planned for this level. It is published in "Appendix C" of this book.

QUESTIONS AND EXERCISES

1. Why are basic word lists essential in the learning of a language?

2. Discuss the differences between Thorndike's approach and Ogden's approach in the study of word lists. Which of these approaches do you regard as best suited to the needs of Hebrew instruction in this country? Why?

3. To what extent is Harper's study of occurrence frequency useful in the teaching of Hebrew in our schools? How would Rieger's study be helpful? What is the difference in their approaches? What are the inadequacies in both these approaches for the purpose of Hebrew methodology in this country?

4. How can the word list approach be employed to improve the efficiency of Hebrew instruction in our schools?

5. Evaluate the vocabularies in the first ten lessons of two popular primers in terms of the word list given

in "Appendix B." To what extent are the words in the primers wisely chosen?

6. In the light of these evaluations do you feel that these primers meet the need of preparing our pupils adequately for the study of the Bible or for the biblical texts of *Bereshit* or *Shemot*? How could you overcome the inadequacies of the textbooks in regard to Bible-readiness?

7. Analyze one of the accepted primers to find out the density of new vocabulary, i. e., the ratio of new words to running words. How closely does this ratio approximate the desired standard of "about forty running words for every new word introduced during the first year" (Gates)? How could this handicap be partly remedied?

8. Examine one or more of the stories of each series or the supplementary reading materials suggested in chapter VII to determine to what degree the basic vocabulary is wisely chosen in the light of the criteria of the word list in "Appendix C."

9. How could word lists be used in the classroom as an aid in the building and enrichment of vocabulary?

REFERENCES

Cole, R. D. and Tharp, J. B. — *Modern Foreign Languages and Their Teaching*, Appleton, Chapter VI.
Handschin, C. H. — *Modern Language Teaching*, World Book Co., Chapter VII.

CHOMSKY, WILLIAM — "Vocabulary as a Basis for Hebrew Methodology," in *Jewish Education*, IX, 2.
——— "A Basic Vocabulary in Hebrew for First Three Years," in *Jewish Education*, VII, I.
FIFE, R. H. — *A Summary of Reports on the Modern Foreign Languages*, pp. 188–203.
GATES, A. I. — *Interest and Ability in Reading*, Macmillan, Chapter I.
HUSE, H. R. — *Reading and Speaking Foreign Languages*, Chapel Hill, 1945, Chapter VI.
HARPER, W. R. — *Hebrew Vocabularies*, Second Edition, Chicago, 1882.
SCHARFSTEIN, ZEVI — שילה, דרכי למוד לשוננו, Chapter IX.
WEST, M — *Language in Education*, Longmans, Green, Chapters V–VII.

CHAPTER X

THE TEACHING OF HEBREW GRAMMAR

THE NEED OF A KNOWLEDGE OF GRAMMAR
IN THE STUDY OF HEBREW

Few will deny that a knowledge of grammar is essential to an intelligent appreciation of a language, both for the purpose of reading and for effective use in oral and wirtten expression. This is particularly true in the case of the Hebrew language, which is, on the one hand, the vehicle of an ancient culture and of archaic forms of self-expression; and, on the other hand, a regenerated instrumentality for modern usage in everyday life-situations, especially in Palestine. Furthermore, Hebrew, like the other Semitic languages, is a consonantal language; that is, the basal meaning is inherent in the consonants, while variations of vowels determine grammatical modifications of meaning, such as are generally rendered in European languages by entirely different words. For example, the English words *bat, bait, bite, bet, bate, but, boat, beat, boot, about* have nothing in common either in etymology or in meaning, although they all have a common consonantal basis, namely *bt*. On the other hand, the Hebrew consonantal stem קדש carries the basal meaning in all its manifold derivational and inflectional changes. Hence, a knowledge of Hebrew grammar enables the student of Hebrew to get along on a comparatively small basic vocabulary, while ignorance of grammar necessitates the mastery of an inordinately large vocabulary.

Yet, the results in the teaching of this subject, whether in the elementary grades or in the advanced departments, are far from satisfactory. The achievements are not at all commensurate with the amount of time and effort invested, with the result that a feeling of skepticism on the worthwhileness of this study has become widespread among teachers of Hebrew. There is apparent confusion as to methodology, as well as a dearth of proper text materials, in this subject.

The Problem of Content and Method

There are two aspects to this problem: (1) the question of what to teach in this subject, how much grammatical material to cover on the various levels of the pupils' progress in the language, and (2) how to teach this material on each of the levels.

In the field of general pedagogy, the following two principles are offered in regard to the teaching of grammar, whether of native or of foreign languages: (1) Grammatical rules and principles should be taught only as need arises. (2) The frequency with which grammatical items and peculiarities are encountered in the language determines their claim to priority in the grammar course. In other words, the minds of the pupils should not be glutted with rules and principles which they do not need and cannot appreciate now, but which they may need and appreciate at some future time, at a later stage in their growth in language power. Only those grammatical elements should be taught at each stage, which occur most frequently in the reading materials at the particular level of the pupils' progress in the language, and the explanation of which will aid in furthering this progress. Obviously, whatever grammar is taught at any stage should be directly related to the vocabulary of the pupils at this stage. Verbs conjugated, nouns inflected, etc., should be such as are comprised in the respective wordlists of the pupils.

Furthermore, it must be remembered that the mere knowledge of a rule, or a paradigm, is no more a guaranty of its being observed or practised in actual usage than is the knowledge of rules of conduct a guaranty of proper conduct in actual life-situations. The proper functioning of a rule, in grammar as well as in conduct, is contingent upon the following conditions: (1) The practice must be carried on in lifelike situations; namely, in situations which resemble those of real life, in which the particular rule is expected to function. (2) The practice should be adequately motivated, emotionally colored, and its need should be recognized and experienced by the pupils. For this reason rules in grammar should be reduced to a minimum and should be clearly presented, explained and amplified by means of text materials, which furnish examples and illustrations. A long list of rules, dogmatically presented, can neither be memorized and retained, nor is there any probability that the retention of these rules will lead to proper usage.

The study of grammar is, accordingly, merely a phase of the study of language. The two studies are closely interlinked, and no clear and sharp distinction can be drawn between them. The extent and nature of the grammatical material needed at the various levels of the language course are determined by the objectives of the course. When the aim of the course is a reproductive knowledge of the language, that is, the ability to speak and write the language, a much greater amount of grammatical knowledge and higher degree of mastery are required than where the aim is merely a recognition or reading knowledge. For example, the ability to identify the gender of certain nouns, or the conjugation of certain verbs, or the knowledge of the differences in the vocalization of the definite article (ה' הידיעה), in Hebrew, is of little help in facilitating reading comprehension, but is distinctly helpful for conversational and composition purposes.

Thus the course in grammar may be divided roughly into three categories or levels: the primary, the intermediate and the advanced levels.

Content and Method in the Elementary Grades

Since the reading materials generally incorporated in the readers for the primary grades are, on the whole, simple in structure and relatively free of grammatical intricacies, the amount of grammatical knowledge needed for recognition or reading purposes is very limited. The recognition of grammatical forms is largely a matter of vocabulary study. It is, for example, unnecessary to know, at this level, that ספר is a *Pi'el* conjugation of the stem ספר, the *Kal* of which is סָפַר, etc. The word ספר is simply a new word and is related to סָפַר in the same manner as is ספור to סָפַר. Each has to be learned as a separate unit, although the etymological kinship may sometimes be pointed out, especially whenever the words are related in meaning. All the grammatical knowledge needed at this stage is the ability to recognize the suffixes in the nouns by which to identify gender, number and pronominal relationships, as well as the prefixes and suffixes in the verbs by which tenses and persons are indicated. Only such grammatical elements, the knowledge of which facilitates reading power, are admissible at this stage.

In the intermediate stage, when the pupils begin the study of biblical texts and of classical selections from modern Hebrew, the course in Hebrew grammar must be extended to include also the study of the conjugations. The complicated grammatical forms of these texts, especially the forms with the so-called *Waw-*Consecutive, whereby a future tense is changed to a past and vice versa, make the study of the conjugations necessary even for recognition purposes. Otherwise the number of "new" words to be learned will be unduly multiplied. But here, likewise, the criteria of need and occurrence-frequency mentioned above, should be employed in the arrangement and inclusion of grammatical facts to be studied. Thus, for example, no verb in the Hebrew language occurs in all the conjugations, while some conjugations, like the *Pu'al* and *Hoph'al*, are very rare altogether. Of all the 344 verbs that occur with high frequency in the Bible (25–5,000 times), there are only 17 that occur 5 times and over in the *Pu'al* and 12 in the *Hoph'al*. It is, therefore, wasteful to construct and to study conjugations and verb-forms which are rare or purely hypothetical, occurring only in grammar books or in the imagination of grammarians.

The same is true in the case of the feminine plural in the future tense (e. g., תִּכְתֹּבְנָה). This cumbersome form was on the wane even in the late biblical period, and is dropped entirely in mishnaic literature. In the

Bible we find numerous examples, where a masculine plural replaces the feminine plural in the future. In *Shir ha-Shirim*, for instance, there are ten cases of the "masculine" forms against three of the "feminine." Why burden our children's minds with archaic forms which have lost their functional character in the course of the development of the language?

In both the primary and intermediate grades, the study of grammar, like the study of vocabulary and idiom, is largely a matter of habituation. The grammatical rules and principles have meaning and value only when they function spontaneously and automatically, whether in the process of recognition, as in the case of reading, or of reproduction, as in writing and speaking. Hence the method of teaching grammar in these grades must be based on the principles of habituation; namely, concentration on a few elements at a time, much drill and practice, adequate motivation and practice in functional situations in terms of the objectives of language study.

The inductive approach is generally recommended by modern educators, on the basis of experimentation and observation, as the most effective. By this approach, the pupils are exposed to numerous examples in oral and reading situations, in which certain grammatical elements are stressed until they become ingrained in the mind, then the rule governing these elements is brought out, formulated and explained.

Whenever possible the pupils should be guided to evolve and formulate the rule themselves on the basis of the examples studied. Consequently, the text material in language or in Bible must be used as the basis for the study of the grammar. Examples and illustrations should be drawn from these texts which lead up to a certain generalization or principle, the significance of which the pupils can be made to appreciate, since it deepens their insight into the structure of the language, gives them a feeling of mastery and power in usage, and enables them at the same time to read their Hebrew text with greater intelligence and appreciation. However, the teacher must not lose sight of the fact that grammatical analysis is only a means, while understanding and appreciation are the end.

In order to apply and reinforce the grammatical principles learned, exercises should be provided in some form of connected discourse and not in the form of isolated words or sentences. Drill is most effective when the elements drilled on are organized and integrated into a lifelike and meaningful pattern. There is a variety of exercises of such contextual types. Thus, for example, after having learned a certain number of conjugations, the reading selection of the text may be examined and the verb-forms classified in accordance with an outline of conjugations which may be placed on the blackboard or distributed to the students in mimeographed sheets. Similarly, students

TEACHING OF HEBREW GRAMMAR 177

may be asked to rewrite a selection from the reading matter, in which they should be asked to change the tenses; or the gender, person, and number of the characters. Questions on content may also be so designed as to call for responses in which the application of the grammatical principles learned may be brought into play. Completion and matching exercises, such as are found in some workbooks, putting these principles into operation are also recommendable, examples of which are given below.

First Grade Type

I. Fill in for הַיַלְדָה and הַיְלָדִים what the sentence below says for הַיֶלֶד. Choose from the מִלִים below. The first is an example.

הַיֶלֶד בּוֹכֶה	הַיֶלֶד רוֹאֶה	הַיֶלֶד קוֹרֵא
הַיַלְדָה _____	הַיַלְדָה _____	הַיַלְדָה קוֹרְאָה
הַיְלָדִים _____	הַיְלָדִים _____	הַיְלָדִים _____
יֶלֶד טוֹב	יֶלֶד גָדוֹל	יֶלֶד חָכָם
יַלְדָה _____	יַלְדָה _____	יַלְדָה _____
יְלָדִים _____	יְלָדִים _____	יְלָדִים _____

מִלִים

טוֹבִים	בּוֹכִים	טוֹבָה	רוֹאָה
חֲכָמִים	רוֹאִים	חֲכָמָה	גְדוֹלָה
קוֹרְאִים	גְדוֹלִים	קוֹרְאָה	בּוֹכָה

Ḥumash Grade Type

כתבו על יד כל עבר פשוט (simple past) את המספר של המלה המקבילה (corresponding) בעבר מהופך (converted past), על פי הדוגמה (example) הראשונה.

עָבָר מְהוּפָּךְ		עָבָר פָּשׁוּט
א. וָיַחֲלֹם	ו	שָׁכַחְתִּי
ב. וָאֶחֱלֹם	―――	חָלַם
ג. וַיַּחְלְמוּ	―――	זָכְרוּ
ד. וַנַחֲלֹם	―――	שָׁכְחוּ
ה. וַיִּשְׁכְּחוּ	―――	חָלַמְתִּי
ו. וָאֶשְׁכַּח	―――	זָכַר
ז. וַיִּזְכֹּר	―――	זָכַרְתִּי
ח. וַיִּזְכְּרוּ	―――	שָׁכַח
ט. וַנִּזְכֹּר	―――	שָׁכַחְנוּ
י. וָאֶזְכֹּר	―――	זָכַרְנוּ
י"א. וַנִּשְׁכַּח	―――	חָלְמוּ
י"ב. וַיִּשְׁכַּח	―――	חָלַמְנוּ

It is, of course, inadvisable to interrupt the reading or study of the text with grammatical explanations and drills, except in an incidental manner. The lesson in grammar should be set apart for a special period. Comprehension and appreciation of content involve different mental processes from those involved in grammatical analysis. The reading attitude is definitely hampered by diverting attention to word-forms and grammatical details. These two language activities, while mutually helpful, are mutually distracting when practiced simultaneously.

Content and Method in the Advanced Stages

The third stage in the study of grammar calls for a more comprehensive course and a more rational, rather than empirical, approach. But here, likewise, much of the grammatical material generally included in our texts in Hebrew grammar should be discarded. Some of the grammatical rules are obsolete, others are baseless and mere figments of the imagination of grammarians.

For example, the rules on the distinction between long and short vowels and between the silent and vocal *Shewa* are artificial, non-functional, and are based on misconceptions. The accepted distinction between five long and five short vowels was devised by Joseph and his son David Kimḥi, prominent Hebrew grammarians of the 12th and 13th centuries, under the influence of the Latin languages employed in the Provence where they lived. Their predecessors knew of no such quantitative distinction, nor is there any evidence from any other ancient sources which may substantiate the existence of such a phonetic distinction in the traditional Jewish pronunciations. This distinction is artificial and alien to the phonology of Hebrew and of the other Semitic languages, and has never been put into actual practice except by pedantic grammarians.

The same applies to the distinction between the silent and vocal *Shewa*. The erroneous distinction between the long and short vowels led the Kimḥis to the error of distinguishing between silent and vocal *Shewas*. Since the unaccented "long" vowels, according to their system, could not occur in a closed syllable, the *Shewa* following these vowels had to be regarded as vocal. But the Hebrew grammarians preceding the Kimḥis knew of no such vocal *Shewa* and there is sufficient evidence to prove that masoretic tradition never intended to have this *Shewa* sounded. The only vocal *Shewa* recorded by pre-Kimḥian grammarians are those which must, of phonetic necessity, be sounded, such as the *Shewa* which is not preceded by any vowel as in the ב or ת of בְּלָכְתְּךָ, or that in a consonant doubled by a *Dagesh* as in the ב in נבאו. But no rules are needed in these cases.

To be sure, at some early stage in the history of the language, all these cases with "vocal *Shewa*" were fully sounded, but so were also the cases with "silent *Shewa*." But modern grammar is descriptive rather than prescriptive. Its task is to record the evolutionary changes in language and to seek to explain them, but not to prescribe the form that these changes should take and to accept or reject them. Since the Hebrew language has never ceased to live its normal phonetic life in the tradition of the Jewish people, especially in their Houses of Prayer and of Study, the latest phonetic changes in the evolutionary process must be accepted as valid. There is ample proof that the process of "silencing" the consonants now having "vocal *Shewa*" goes, in some cases, as far back as the talmudic period. In modern times the "vocal *Shewa*" is ignored even in the living speech of Palestine, despite the efforts of pedantic grammarians.

The empirical treatment of grammatical data should give way to a rational approach. The advanced student in Hebrew is interested not only in the "how" of linguistic facts but also in the "why." Principles of Hebrew grammar should be explained to him in the light of historical development and general linguistic science. He should know, for example, something about the history of the Hebrew language; its origin and relation to the other Semitic languages. He should get some idea about the Masorah and its influence on biblical exegesis and grammar, about the history of the alphabet and of the vowel-system, about the outstanding Hebrew pronunciations and their origin, about the distinctive syntactical characteristics of biblical Hebrew, mishnaic Hebrew and modern Hebrew, and so on. Such an approach will promote the student's interest in the language and will enhance his power of appreciation of it.

Furthermore, at this stage, even where the reading objective is adopted, reproductive or functional ability is a desideratum and should be cultivated. The grammatical principles should be exercised and applied in oral and written expression. Theoretical knowledge must be translated into actual usage and power, in all the various aspects of the language.

QUESTIONS AND EXERCISES

1. List, on the basis of actual observation and experience, some typical examples of grammatical errors made in speech and in writing by children (a) in the primary grades and (b) in the more advanced grades. How could these errors be eliminated most effectively?

2. "The objectives in learning a language determine the amount and the content of the grammar course, as well as the method and procedure." What are the implications of this statement for the teaching of grammar (a) in our primary and elementary grades and (b) in the more advanced grades?

3. Examine the first 10 lessons in a series of primers for the first, second and third years to see the grammatical difficulties presented to the pupils in each of them. List these difficulties.

4. Examine the workbooks attached to some of the modern primers. To what extent do these workbooks provide for the mastery of the grammatical difficulties?

5. What elements of grammar are particularly needed to facilitate comprehension in reading Hebrew? Which are essential for purposes of speaking and writing?

6. What is meant by the Inductive Approach in teaching grammar? How does it differ from the traditional Deductive or Formal-Grammar Approach? What is the place of each of these approaches in the language course of study in our schools?

7. In the light of your findings of the typical difficulties in grammar encountered by the pupils in the primary and elementary grades, investigate some of the formal grammar texts prepared for these grades and express your opinion as to their effectiveness. To what extent do these texts help the pupils overcome their specific difficulties?

REFERENCES

CHUBB, P. — *The Teaching of English*, Macmillan, Chapter XII.
COLE-THARP — *Modern Foreign Languages and Their Teaching*, Chapter IX.
HANDSCHIN, C H. — *Modern Language Teaching*, 1940, Chapter VI.
McMURRY, C. A. — *Special Methods in Language*, Macmillan, Chapters I–V.
SCHARFSTEIN, ZEVI — שילה, דרכי למוד לשוננו, Chapter XVIII.
SHREVE, F — *Psychology of the Teaching of English*, Christopher Publishing House, 1941, Chapter IV.

Chapter XI

THE TEACHING OF BIBLE IN OUR ELEMENTARY GRADES

The Significance of the Bible

The Hebrew curriculum in our schools is clearly Bible-centered. The Hebrew language taught in our primary grades is generally designated as "preparatory to the Bible." Many authors of Hebrew textbooks for primary grades lay special emphasis on the claim that their text-books are designed to prepare the pupils for the study of the Bible in Hebrew.

This is as it should be. The Bible is, without a doubt, a basic Book in Jewish life and Jewish literature. Consequently, it should also be a basic Book in Jewish education. The pedagogic value of Bible study from a religious, ethical, social and national point of view can hardly be overestimated. Through this Book our pupils may come into possession of the most significant and profoundest experiences of their people. By studying it they may acquire the ideas, techniques and values of the past, which have served us as incalculable resources of guidance for the evaluation and control of current experiences.

However, it is not safe to assume that the mere study of the Bible text, or familiarity with its content, will guarantee the acquisition of the loyalties, insights and motives, which we deem so valuable. Recent investigations and studies show little, if any, connection between knowledge of the Bible and any of the character traits that such knowledge is presumed to foster. A superficial examination of our own efforts in Bible teaching and of the results achieved will suffice to dispel any illusions that we may have in this connection. We need but ask ourselves: to what extent do we succeed in cultivating in our pupils the desire and the ability to study the Bible independently? How many of our pupils, who have studied the Bible with us, have either the interest or the ability to continue this study of their own accord, after graduation, or after having completed their schooling? In the final analysis, a desire to continue and to grow in the study of a certain subject or in the practice of a skill remains probably the most definite standard by which the efficiency of methods of instruction may be measured. If our pupils studying the Bible fail to develop a desire and an ability to continue this study, how much of what they have learned will eventually be retained? How can we expect, under these circumstances, to have this Book serve for them as a source of inspiration, stimulation and guidance?

Difficulties in Teaching Bible

What may account for our failure thus far to achieve our aim in Bible instruction?

The process of teaching Bible to children, especially in the original Hebrew, is strewn with many difficulties, difficulties of content and style, of concepts and ideas, as well as of language. It is not within the province of this text to discuss these difficulties. However, since the Bible is being taught in the elementary grades and in view of the significance of this subject in our curriculum, even in our elementary grades, some comments and recommendations will be made here.

It cannot be emphasized too strongly and too frequently that our pupils approaching the study of the Bible must be more or less adequately prepared linguistically. There can be no thought of training our children to study the Bible with appreciative understanding as long as language barriers exist. A study of literature, interrupted by vocabulary drills and explanations, is not conducive to genuine appreciation. The moment drill and drudgery enter, appreciation leaves. It should be quite obvious that when the attention of the pupils and teacher is focused on the study of vocabulary and idiom, no desirable effect on the cultivation of literary appreciation or on the building of character may be expected, however valuable the content may be. Such a study of the Bible is nothing more than a study of the biblical dictionary.

As an illustration of the linguistic difficulties which are encountered in the teaching of the Bible, even in the accepted abridged editions, the following figures may be revealing. The book of *Bereshit*, Scharfstein's abridged edition, comprises 1,069 basic words. Of this number, 411 words, or about 38 per cent, occur only once, while only 332 words, or 31 per cent, occur with a frequency of five and above. The situation is even more unsatisfactory, in regard to recurrence-frequency, in *Shemot*, in the same edition. Evidently, language texts with such low rates of recurrence-frequency will present a difficult problem in language methodology, especially in the case of texts, where the appreciation of the content is the chief objective.

The redeeming feature in this situation is the fact that these 332 words in *Bereshit*, although constituting only 31 per cent of the total basic words, actually represent 88 per cent of the total running words in the book. However, several factors must be taken into account. First, there is no regularity in the spread of the vocabulary load, with the result that some chapters have a disproportionate number of new words. Secondly, the large number and variety of grammatical formations, as well as idiomatic expressions, are too complicated and difficult to master. Thirdly, the preparatory vocabulary learned by our pupils in the primary grades is in most cases, as demonstrated by objective tests, but vaguely mastered, and additional reviews are needed to fix these words more firmly in their minds. But the Bible texts offer very little opportunity for such reviews. Under the circumstances the Bible instruction degenerates, of necessity, into mere verbalism, and the Bible text comes to be regarded by the pupils as a book of language and drill exercises rather than a book of inspirational content.

A Possible Solution

What is the possible solution? How may we render the teaching of the Bible capable of achieving the desired results?

A primary requisite for an appreciative study of the Bible is, of course, a firm grasp of the essential biblical vocabulary and the acquisition of facility and interest in reading sense-material within this vocabulary. Now, as was pointed out previously, 332 basic words constitute 88 per cent of the total running words in the book of *Bereshit*. But what is even more significant is the fact that only 186 of these basic words, occurring ten times and above in this book, represent 80 per cent of the total running words of the book. Since these 186 words are almost all such as occur with high frequency in the entire Bible (100–5,000 times) it may be assumed that they are basic in about the same proportion in any other narrative part of the Bible. To teach such a small number of words effectively and thoroughly should be a very simple matter, since most of our primers, even of the first year, include about twice this number of words, many of which are, however, extraneous in terms of Bible readiness and remain in the child's mind, if they are learned at all, as so much dead weight. The success in pursuing the study of the Bible will be obviously determined by the extent to which we can control the teaching of Hebrew, in the primary grades, in terms of this selected vocabulary load, and by the degree in which we may succeed in cultivating facility and interest in sense-reading, by means of extensive practice in reading interesting materials within this vocabulary.

But careful discrimination should also be exercised in the selection of biblical materials during the early stages of Bible study. The most promising method of selection would probably be by a sort of cycle approach according to which the Bible is to be taught in the form of cycles instead of segments, as is the practice at present. Each cycle should comprise such materials from the entire range of biblical literature, as are suited and adaptable, from the standpoint of character value, interest and language, to the particular level of maturity and linguistic preparation of the pupils.

An attempt to adapt the story of Joseph (chapters XXXVII–L in *Bereshit*) to pupils of the third grade in Hebrew was made by the writer, with the collaboration of Mr. Abraham Segal (ילקוט ספורי מקרא,

יוסף ואחיו, 1938). With very slight modifications in the text, such as did no violence to the original content and style, it was possible to reduce the proportion of new words, in terms of the three-year basic wordlist of the Associated Talmud Torahs[1] from an average of about 12 per cent to an average of less than 3 per cent of the total running words. The grammatical difficulties were likewise simplified to a considerable degree. That such adaptations would result in an increased interest in the Bible and in a desire to continue its study can hardly be doubted.

In brief, the proposed biblical anthology should include, in the writer's estimation, in addition to the thirteen chapters from *Bereshit*, some ten additional chapters from the same book, centering around the life of Abraham and Isaac. A good beginning in this book is the portion of לך־לך, chapter XII, where we meet for the first time with a real historical hero. Selections from the other books of the Bible should comprise the following selections: (1) About twelve chapters from *Shemot*, relating the story of the life of Moses and of the Exodus; (2) About six chapters from *Bamidbar*, covering the stories of the *Meraglim*, of Korah and of Balaam; (3) About four chapters from *Joshua* relative to the conquest of Canaan; (4) About

---

[1] Cf. above, Chapter IX.

eight chapters from *Shoftim*, covering the stories of Deborah, Gideon and Samson; (5) About twenty-four chapters from *Samuel I and II*, dealing with the lives of Samuel, Saul and David; (6) About seven chapters from *Kings*, covering the activities of Solomon and Elijah; (7) The book of *Ruth*, and also some selections from *Esther*. This would constitute a total of some 90 chapters that could be covered in about two years. After having covered these most interesting stories of the Bible in this manner, the pupils should have a linguistic and an appreciative background, as well as the curiosity, to read the narrative and other simple parts of the Bible in the original, perhaps also, in the case of the *Humash*, with a sprinkling of *Rashi*. The pedagogic possibilities of *Rashi's* commentaries on the *Humash* have, unfortunately, not been sufficiently exploited in our modern schools. The prophetic and the poetic selections of the Bible will constitute the third cycle, but this cycle is not in the province of the elementary department.

The argument that by such an approach the continuity of the stories will be interrupted is untenable, since by the time the children reach the third or fourth year in the Hebrew school, they are familiar with the Bible stories and legends which they study in their history courses. The teacher in Bible should, of course, draw upon this information in order to provide the connecting links and the historical and legendary background, which may serve to elucidate and amplify the material in the Bible texts.

Conclusion

To sum up, the advantages of such an approach would be as follows:

1. It would provide for our pupils an opportunity to read and study with appreciative understanding and interest simple and wholesome Bible stories in the original biblical language and style.

2. It would equip the pupils with study habits and with abilities needed in effective and independent work, thus liberating the pupils progressively from teacher guidance and dependence. Much of the material in this simplified form could be read and studied with very little assistance from the teacher.

3. It would provide for adequate review without the monotony of drill and repetition. The pupils would cover the same texts more than once, without having the feeling that they are merely going over the same ground.

4. It would implant in the pupils interests and desires which would make for continuity and growth in the study of the Bible.

5. It will give pupils who stay in the school for a limited number of years the opportunity to get an

integrated impression of biblical content. Under the present circumstances very few children ever get to the reading of the narrative portions in the books of the Early Prophets.

It will, of course, be objected that many of our pupils will never get to the "real" Bible by such an approach. But what gain is there in the study of a few chapters of the real Bible, if concomitantly with this laborious study is acquired an aversion for the Bible? Actually, these pupils merely study the words of the Bible without catching its spirit or message. Would it not be far better, if as a result of the approach suggested here, the children who are likely to drop out would develop an interest, which might pique their curiosity later on to dip, of their own accord, into the sources of the real Bible? Furthermore, a more interesting approach in the study of the Bible will most likely result in a firmer holding power on our pupils.

As was stated previously there is no attempt to discuss here exhaustively, or even adequately, the various phases of Bible methodology. Such a discussion will have to be reserved for another occasion. Essentially, the methodology of the Bible in Hebrew, especially in the elementary grades, differs little from that of language and literature, and the procedure and techniques recommended for the teaching of these subjects will apply also to the teaching of the Bible. However, since the Bible is being taught in our elementary grades and since the results are generally far from satisfactory, there is a need for some specific recommendations, which may be found helpful. These recommendations will be presented in the subsequent chapter.

Chapter XII

SPECIFIC SUGGESTIONS FOR THE TEACHING OF BIBLE

Very rarely do our elementary schools reach the stages of teaching any but the narrative portions of the Bible in Hebrew. Hence, the subsequent suggestions will be restricted to methods and devices of teaching these portions, although some of these suggestions may apply as well to the teaching of any other portions.

Steps in the Bible Lesson

In planning and preparing his lesson, the teacher of Bible must bear in mind the following considerations and principles.

I. *Subject Matter* — Familiarize yourself thoroughly with the subject matter to be taught. The accepted meanings of vocabularies, idioms and expressions should be clearly and precisely comprehended, so that they can be just as clearly and precisely transmitted to the pupils. Be independent of the book. Acquaint yourself also with the historical and legendary backgrounds of the particular lesson. Select and bring to the attention of your pupils such of these materials as will help to enliven, enrich and render more meaningful the lesson taught. The traditional interpretations and legends such as may be found in Rashi's commentaries and in other sources often add descriptive details and picturesque situations, which expand the artistic canvass, as it were, and lend the concise biblical narrative more concreteness and more vividness for the inexperienced and immature mental vision of our pupils.

II. *Aim* — Decide on major and minor aims for the lesson both in general and in specific terms. Choose some significant elements in the lesson which deserve stressing, whether in the nature of important facts of information, or of attitudes, appreciations and ideals; or of significant vocabularies, idioms and expressions. You should also know pretty definitely and precisely the details of information, the particular ethical principles or ideals, or the specific vocabularies and idioms that you expect the pupils to learn as the outcome of this lesson.

III. *Method* — The method should, of course, be adapted and designed with the view to achieving the aims of the lesson. If there are vocabularies and expressions that need stressing, provide for adequately motivated drill. Create and utilize opportunities for practice. Refer to the available stock of games and devices and select those that fit your particular purpose.

If the lesson lends itself to the development of ideas and the understanding of facts and events, you should endeavor to provoke and stimulate reflective thinking. Prepare some pivotal and thought-provoking questions for this purpose. In the case of a lesson for attitudes, appreciations and ideals, direct your appeal chiefly to the emotional and imaginative background of your pupils. Try to enlist emotional participation and experience by making the lesson picturesque and vivid, and by stressing the dramatic or ethical elements, as the case may be.

IV. *Materials* — Have on hand the needed text materials, as well as whatever illustrative aids may be obtained which are likely to make the lesson more intelligible, vivid and concrete, such as maps, charts, graphs, pictures, and so on. Such materials are plentiful and available. The ambitious and resourceful teacher will not, however, depend entirely on the ready and manufactured materials. He will stimulate and guide his pupils to prepare such materials of their own. These materials may be inferior artistically to those on the market, but they can be made to serve our educational purposes much more effectively.

V. *Procedure* — The specific steps in the lessons may be broadly stated as follows:

1. *Motivation* — Every lesson should, of course, start and proceed with the momentum of a strong motivation. Otherwise, the lesson is liable to degenerate into

a perfunctory exercise carried on on a low level of effort and attention. The following are some of the steps that may be employed as sources of motivation:

a. Adapt the material to the experience of the pupils. Old related knowledge and experience should be recalled and utilized as a background for new learning. Context of previously learned lessons should be reviewed to explain the meaning of vocabularies and expressions. Domestic and environmental experiences, as well as familiar facts of information, should be employed as a link for the new information. New facts should be provided when needed as a basis for understanding and appreciating the particular selection. For example, the story of Eliezer and Rebekkah at the well may fail to produce any clear imagery, or it may evoke distorted imagery in the minds of our modern urban children, who have never seen a well or girls drawing water. A picture in this instance would be helpful. A verbal description or explanation will also be needed for further clarification. Similarly, the concept of famine and all it connotes in the migration of the patriarchs into Egypt will probably be entirely alien to our well-fed American children without an adequate explanation of the differences in climate, etc. Failure to appreciate the significance of water in Palestine may completely obscure the meaning of the struggle for wells in the Bible stories. The full and lofty meaning of some of the Ten Commandments is

SPECIFIC SUGGESTIONS FOR TEACHING BIBLE

entirely lost on children who have not had the experiential background necessary for its appreciation. In all such cases the teacher must prepare the pupils, equip them, at least, vicariously, by means of pictorial materials and adequate explanations and illustrations with the necessary background; and the vocabulary employed by the teacher and in the text must of course be crystal clear to the children.

b. Enlist the natural interest of children. As far as possible the lesson should be organized around interests common to all children and around activities in which children normally like to engage. All normal and healthy children like to play games, to listen to stories, to act out and dramatize situations and happenings, to draw, to paste, to label, to solve puzzles, etc. Plan your lesson with the view to incorporating as many of these activities as possible, but in such a manner as to lead to the desired learning results. Refer to Chapter VI for suggestions of games and activities.

c. Put your pupils in a problem-solving state of mind. Create and initiate problems, difficulties which can be solved through the material to be presented. Stimulate purposeful activities leading through learning situations involving information, practice and study. Set before them some goal or purpose which children may regard as desirable. Guide them to realize the need of mastering the particular vocabularies and text materials as necessary steps to the desired ends. Give the pupils a clear view of these goals or ends to be attained in consequence of the mastery of these vocabularies and text materials. These ends may be: the execution of a dramatic project or a festival program, playing a game, finding out "what's coming next" in the story, a higher mark in the group or individual progress chart, the chance to communicate an idea or fact, and so on. The latter, for example, can be utilized effectively in the teaching of Bible stories, the contents of which are familiar to the children from their study of history. Prod them by means of appropriate questions, preferably in Hebrew, to tell you what they know about the particular story. Guide them to use as much as possible the Hebrew of the text in their answers. Present and drill on the new vocabulary while they are eager to tell you all they know. Then have them read the text and compare the story in the text with that related orally by them.

d. Remove all difficulties in thought and in language before reading the material in the text. The reading in the book should be, as far as possible, a smooth continuous activity, uninterrupted by too many questions and by laborious drill. Otherwise, the reading will fail to produce an integrated complete impression. No more appreciation will result from a dissecting attitude of mind in the reading of literary material than from observing a picture hacked into small parts.

Furthermore, it is not advisable to attach the tedium of drill and practice to the text of the Bible, since we are endeavoring to cultivate a continued and abiding interest in the reading and study of this Book. Whatever drill or practice is needed should either precede or follow the reading of the selection in the text.

2. *Presentation* — As the first step in the reading of the selection in the text, it may be advisable to have the teacher read it first, especially in the case of selections where the dramatic element is prominent. The interpretative reading of the teacher will help to bring out the dramatic elements and to set an example of proper meaningful reading. The teacher may also intersperse incidental explanations and comprehension-check questions without interrupting the continuity of the reading. For suggestions on reading by the pupils refer to Chapter VI.

3. *Summaries and Reviews* — Material vaguely understood and partly learned easily fades away from memory. The elements of learning-content, thinly and indistinctly held in the mind, somehow become mutually confusing, and any degree of lasting retention is impossible in such a case. Hence, provision must be made for adequate summaries and reviews, in order to clinch the lesson. A sufficient number of repetitions of the correct response should be insured. Interest should be kept alive by varying drill situations, by

creating and utilizing opportunities for the use of the newly learned expressions and idioms, and by occasional summaries and restatements.

Leave in the consciousness of your pupils a feeling of having mastered a complete unified whole, so as to lead them to a sense of self-confidence and to a desire for further growth. Summarize or have the pupils summarize, at the end, the important points of the lesson.

4. *Application and Assignment* — Create opportunities for applying the knowledge acquired and attitudes aroused and the language elements learned in some actual and interesting situations. Let it take the character of a "follow-up" assignment growing out of the lesson and serving to give it a sense of reality, vividness and permanence. The following are some examples:

a. Have the pupils select certain parts in the lesson that lend themselves to graphic or pictorial illustrations.

b. Have the children answer questions on the text, or have them prepare a list of questions to ask one another in the class.

c. Have the children select certain phrases or expressions that particularly appeal to them. Let them tell you the reason for their choice. Some of them may be used as memory gems or mottoes.

d. Have them prepare an outline, summary, or synopsis of the selections studied.

e. Let the pupils prepare comparisons of characters,

situations, or events. This may be done on the basis of an outline prepared either by the teacher, or co-operatively by the pupils themselves.

f. Ask the pupils to rework the lesson by introducing imaginary dialogues.

g. Have the pupils write imaginary letters or diaries relating striking incidents in the life of the characters studied; such as: Abraham's departure from his birthplace and his father's home, his battle against the kings who captured Lot, his anxiety and mental struggle when he was ordered to offer his son Isaac as a sacrifice, etc. The lives of the other biblical heroes present similar opportunities.

h. Have them plan and prepare a dramatization or pageant. This may be done cooperatively in the classroom, or the pupils may bring in suggestions individually in writing. Assignments of this type are generally suited for review purposes and are inclusive, covering several lessons.

QUESTIONS AND EXERCISES

Chapters XI and XII

1. Analyze the selections generally included in our abridged texts for elementary grades in terms of (a) their value for character training, (b) their bearing

on problems of the domestic and social environment of the child and (c) their general significance in cultivating Jewish loyalties.

2. Which of the biblical narratives are particularly suited to the tastes and level of intelligence of the children in the elementary grades and which are less suited? For what reason?

3. How can legendary material and traditional commentaries be utilized to complement the text and to adjust the "less suited" materials to the children's level of intelligence, maturity and appreciation? Cite examples.

4. What are some of the typical difficulties encountered in the teaching of Bible to children in the elementary grades with regard (a) to content and (b) to vocabulary and idiom? How could these difficulties be eased or overcome?

5. Make a study of the enrollment in one or more of the schools in your community to discover the preparation of the children in the school, who stay long enough to cover (a) one book of the Bible, (b) two biblical books, and (c) three or more biblical texts. What may be the reasons for this situation?

6. In the light of the evidence obtained from a study of the elimination in the more advanced grades of our schools, is the alleged emphasis on Bible readiness as the main objective of our Hebrew curriculum justifi-

able? Should the emphasis be changed? Are there any other ways of remedying the situation?

7. Select a chapter in one of the narrative biblical texts and organize a lesson plan, indicating specifically the steps in the lesson.

REFERENCES

CAIGER, S. L. — Bible and Spade, Oxford University Press, 1936.
EISENBERG, A. — Teaching Biblical Literature, Bureau of Jewish Education, Cleveland, O. (Mimeograped)
GOITEIN, S. D. — הוראת התנ׳ך בבית הספר, Hebrew University.
KAPLAN, LOUIS L., "A New Approach to the Teaching of Humosh," *Jewish Education*, XV, 2
SCHARFSTEIN, ZEVI — דרכי למוד התנ׳ך, Jewish Theological Seminary, Chapters I–VII.

Chapter XIII

HOW TO TEACH READING IN THE SIDDUR (MECHANICAL READING)

General Considerations

Siddur reading occupies a prominent place in the elementary grades of the Jewish school, both in terms of time and of emphasis. However, the possibilities of the *Siddur* as an anthology of sacred poetry, of ethical concepts, of religious ideals and national aspirations, are rarely exploited in our schools, especially in the elementary grades. In these grades the *Siddur* is used mostly as a means of training pupils in mechanical reading and in participation in Synagogue services.

A discussion of the broader aspects of *Siddur* methodology is, therefore, outside of the scope of this text. The treatment of this subject will, of necessity, be limited here, in the main, to the mechanical or functional aspects, which are the chief concern of the teacher in the elementary grades.

The term "Mechanical Reading" generally employed for this type of reading means, strictly speaking, conversion of written or printed symbols into sounds. The comprehension of the material "read" is not called for or stressed. The pupil reads with the consciousness that the sound is the thing, and this is what he looks for. The value of this type of "reading" is highly questionable on pedagogic or even religious grounds. It serves no purpose and does not arouse or cultivate desirable emotional responses. This humdrum, listless and perfunctory reading is certainly not likely to implant the sense of love and reverence for the prayerbook which we are endeavoring to inculcate in our children.

There is, however, definitely a place for the teaching of *Siddur* reading even in the primary grades, and provision can and should be made for it in the course of study of these grades. The chief objective in teaching this type of reading in these grades is to enable the child to follow and participate in the services in the synagogue or the Junior Congregation. Only such selections should be taught in the primary grades as are most frequently chanted or recited in the synagogue and in the home. They should be taught in as natural and functional situations as possible; that is, in the manner in which they are used in the synagogue or in the home. The most effective way of learning to pray is by praying in an atmosphere of reverence and solemnity.

The teaching of *Siddur* reading in the primary grades involves different mental processes than in meaningful reading. The assimilative and interpretative processes which are essential in reading for meaning are not involved in *Siddur*-reading, except, perhaps, in the more advanced grades. Hence the two types of reading should be kept distinctly apart from each other and should be taught at different periods.

The assumption prevalent among Hebrew teachers that practice in *Siddur* reading is bound to lead to improvement in the ability to read meaningful Hebrew is without any foundation. Experimental investigations reveal the fact that reading abilities and attitudes differ with the various types of reading materials.[1] There is no such thing as a general reading ability. A person may be an apt reader of newspapers and a poor reader of literary fiction and vice versa. Similarly, one may be trained to read with facility scientific or expository prose and meet with serious difficulties in the reading of poetry, and vice versa. In the writer's experience many of the students trained to read story material in Hebrew are at a loss when they are required to read essays in the same language, even where no vocabulary difficulties are encountered. "A printed page turns out to be ... a source of mass impressions which the active mind begins to organize and arrange with reference to some pattern, which it is trained to work out. If the mind is fitting together the impressions so

---

[1] Cf. Ch. Judd and G. T. Buswell, *Silent Reading*, University of Chicago, 1922, p. 4; also A. I. Gates, *Psychology and Pedagogy of Reading*, 1922, pp. 20–37, and *Teachers College Record*, XX, pp. 98–123.

as to bring into high relief grammatical distinctions, the grouping of words and the distribution of emphasis will be according to one pattern. If the mind is intent on something wholly different from grammar, as, for example, the experiences which the author is trying to picture, the whole mental and physical attitude of the reader will be very different."[2]

In brief, there are as many reading abilities and attitudes as there are types of reading matter, and training in one type does not insure improvement in the reading of the other type. Specific training is necessary in the varied types of reading materials. It is certainly absurd to confuse reading types, so remotely different from each other as the reading of meaningful material and mechanical or *Siddur* reading.

Siddur reading is a process concerned with mastery of words or symbols involving visual-auditory-motor reactions, and involves considerable drill and memorization. Distinct aids in this process are (a) rhythmic sweeps, (b) singing, and (c) games. The initial learning is largely memoriter. It is a "look and say" procedure. Hence the first few selections should be simple — including rhythmic recurrence and repetition of word-forms and sounds, such as *En Kelohenu*, *Adon Olam* and *Shalom Alekhem*. Each selection should be motivated and worked over adequately by means of oral

[2] Ch. Judd and G. T. Buswell, *op. cit.*

drill and blackboard exercises, and through the medium of song and games, before reading it in the *Siddur*. Only after the child has become sufficiently familiarized with the words in the selection, to the extent of being able to identify them in the *Siddur*, should he be asked to recognize them there, thereby experiencing the thrill of discovering "old friends."

The Junior Sabbath Service may serve as a motivation for the reading and study of the selected prayers. These prayers, chants and responses are to be learned and studied for a definite purpose; namely, in order to participate intelligently and appreciatively in the service. Those who achieve a certain level of proficiency in the recitation of given prayers or in the chanting of hymns may be rewarded by the privilege of leading the Junior Congregation in the particular recitation or chant.

In organizing a course of study in the *Siddur* on the primary and elementary level one must bear in mind the following considerations:

1. *Simplicity* — Selections which contain repetitions of sounds, words or phrases take precedence over those where no such repetitions occur. Examples of such simple selections are: אדון עולם, שלום עליכם, אין כאלהינו.

2. *Functional Value* — Prayers and selections that are most frequently recited in the home and in the synagogue, such as קידוש, ברכות הנהנין, שמע, etc., should be given priority.

3. *Chants and Responses* — Selections generally chanted at home and in the synagogue, whether daily, or on the Sabbath, should be studied before those recited only on special occasions or on holidays.

4. *Ceremonial Significance* — Some prayers or recitations have traditionally greater ceremonial significance than others and should be included in the course of study for the earlier grades. Examples: מה נשתנה, *Kiddush* for the holidays, blessings on the Ḥanukkah candles, etc.

In teaching the prayers to older children it is, of course, important to have them understand the meaning of the prayers, their historical background, as well as their national and human values. Younger children are, however, not mature enough for such treatment of the prayers. They may be given the general meaning and interpretation of some of the prayers. They should also be made to realize the significance of identifying themselves with *Kelal Yisrael* by means of reciting prayers which have been recited by Jews all over the world throughout the ages. They should be made to envisage and appreciate the halo of hoary antiquity surrounding these prayers and the historical associations attached to them. The *Shema*, for example, should be associated in the child's mind with the story of Jewish martyrdom ever since the days of Akiba down to the revolt in the Warsaw Ghetto.

Specific Steps of Procedure

1. Begin with such a simple selection of the *Siddur* as אֵין כֵּאלֹהֵינוּ since it contains rhythmic arrangements of sentences, rhyming words and recurrence of word-forms and sounds.

2. Arrange the selections on the board in short lines in accordance with the rhymes, thus:

אֵין כֵּאלֹהֵינוּ

אֵין כַּאדוֹנֵינוּ

etc. Begin with one stanza and add others as the children progress.

3. Teach them to chant or sing it.

4. Have them recognize words with the same final syllables (rhymes) or common initial sounds.

5. Put the phonograms (e.g., נוּ) or common initial sounds on the side of the blackboard and have them learn each as a sound unit.

6. Ask them to find and read the line or word that says (e.g., בָּרוּךְ אֱלֹהֵינוּ).

7. Have several of the pupils in turn conduct this exercise, and organize it in the form of a game.

8. Have a set of syllables or words of the selection arranged promiscuously on the ledge of the blackboard or pinned on the bulletin board, and ask the children to construct various combinations. Or, you may have the words on the blackboard promiscuously arranged,

but numbered, and ask them to make combinations by stating the numbers of the words required.

9. Erase letters and have the children read the missing as well as the remaining part. Then, have them write on the side the missing element. Put back this missing letter and erase another. Proceed in this manner until the entire word or line is reconstructed by the children. Concentrate on a few elements only in each lesson and keep careful record of elements learned.

10. Break up the words into syllables, then into phonic elements (sounds and vowels). Arrange them on the blackboard in perpendicular columns and ask the children to construct various combinations, designating the number.

11. Have children copy at home from a selection in the prayer book words in which certain letters occur. All these exercises should be conducted whenever possible in the form of games.

For further suggestions, see above, Chapter VIII, pages 143-6.

Games and Devices in *Siddur* Reading

The following devices and games may be used to vitalize the practice of *Siddur*-reading:

1. Before starting the reading exercise in the books or on the blackboard, select a number of words that might offer the pupil some difficulty and impede the

practice. Read these words in turn and have some of the pupils find and practice reading them after you, until the visual and auditory symbols become somewhat closely associated in their minds. Analyze them into their elements if necessary and point out outstanding characteristics. The pupil finding the word should indicate it by giving the number of line and position of word, or by reading the word before or after it.

2. Arrange reading exercises under time control. For example: have two teams match each other in straight continuous reading. Assign a certain length of time to each team or a certain number of lines to be covered by each team. Divide the assignment for each team equally among the members of that team. Proceed with the recitation, recording the variable factor, namely, the time taken or lines covered by each team, also number of errors. Members of the same team are allowed to correct one another. In case team א is unable to correct its reader, and a member of team ב is called on to correct, credit is given to team ב.

3. Keep an individual progress chart with the names of all the children on it. Record at each practice period the number of lines read and the number of errors made within a given time, thus giving the child an opportunity to compete with his own record. The teacher may also find it advisable to use a graph in the form of a

READING IN THE SIDDUR

staircase or ladder indicating the status of each pupil in relation to the other pupils in the class with regard to progress in reading. Example:

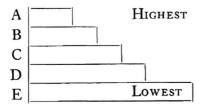

4. Have the two teams opposing each other in the reading contest arrange themselves at opposite ends of the room standing and facing each other. Assign a certain number of lines to each team and divide the assignment among the members of the teams. As soon as a pupil misses a word he leaves his "post" and takes a seat; but is allowed to regain his "post" if he can find and correct a mistake before a member of the opposing team does so. The team having the largest number of members on their "posts," after a given time, wins the game.

5. Let everybody in the class, including the teacher, have a number or letter (preferably Hebrew). A pupil begins to read. In the middle of the reading, the teacher calls on, say, pupil א and this pupil begins to read. Occasionally the teacher calls his own number and begins to read. In the middle of his reading, he stops and calls out ש. All pupils must thus be on

their guard. The general principle in this device is that of the game of fines.

6. Assign a Hebrew letter to each pupil. One pupil is told to read, while the class is instructed that as soon as reader א makes an error, the person following him alphabetically, that is pupil ב, is to continue. If ב overlooks his turn and fails to correct the error, ג takes up the reading, etc. In order to prevent undue excitement on the parts of ג and ד, the instruction should be that upon failure of ב to correct the error, the teacher will signal with a tap or nod or by saying "next." Anyone failing to observe the signal will be eliminated from the particular reading. After a pupil has read a sufficient amount without error, the teacher will call on another pupil out of the alphabetical order.

7. Encourage mutual help and cooperation. Ask one pupil to read while the rest of the class is listening and watching for any errors or words offering special difficulty. After the pupil has read his allotted portion, ask different members of the class to suggest what words the reader should practice in order to improve his reading.

8. Read to discover words which are difficult. As several pupils read, have all the pupils mark down the words they consider difficult. Analyze these words and practice reading them.

9. Assign individual goals — certain prayers which they are to practice individually until they can read

them accurately and within a given length of time. The pupils are called on individually, in their turn, to read the assigned selection. The teacher then directs the pupil to words or parts which require further practice. After the selection is read and meets the required standard of accuracy and speed the next selection is assigned.

10. Certain prayers that are traditionally functional in the Jewish home, such as the *Shema, Kiddush*, etc. should be assigned as practice at home. Credit or some form of recognition may be given to those reported to be practicing the reading of these assignments regularly.

QUESTIONS AND EXERCISES

1. What is the main objective in teaching the *Siddur* in the elementary grades? In the light of this objective and of the principles of "specific practice" (see above p. 40 f.) criticize the procedure of teaching "mechanical reading" generally conducted in our schools.

2. To what extent does "mechanical reading" aid in the development of meaningful reading? What is the evidence in the light of observation and experimentation? What is the psychological difference between the two processes?

3. How would you proceed to organize a "functional" course of study in the *Siddur*? List the prayers you would include in each grade and give your reasons.

4. Is an understanding of the prayers essential to a devotional appreciation of praying? What other factors enter into such an appreciation?

5. What is the particular significance of reciting the traditional prayers in the original Hebrew?

6. How can the reading in the *Siddur* be properly motivated?

7. What are some devices that might vitalize the practice of *Siddur* reading in the classroom?

REFERENCES

GREENBERG, SIMON — *Ideals and Values of the Jewish Prayerbook*, Jewish Theological Seminary.
LEVINE, SAMUEL H. — Manual for the Teaching of Siddur, Bureau of Jewish Education, Cleveland, O., 1942. (Mimeographed)
LIEBMAN, MOSHE — "להוראת הסדור", שבילי החנוך, III, 3.
MILLNER A.— חנוך. על הקריאה בסדור (edited by Z. Scharfstein) II, 3.
SUSSMAN, SAMUEL — "Synagogue Services", The Synagogue Center, June 1941.

Chapter XIV

A TESTING PROGRAM IN HEBREW

The Place of Testing in the Curriculum

In any kind of program or project, successful achievement depends on careful planning. One must have a clear perspective of the aims he wishes to attain and of the direction in which he must head in order to achieve them. He must also have a compass, as it were, by which to be guided and a chart to indicate the progress he is making toward his goal.

We have already discussed the aims and methods in the teaching of Hebrew, as well as the specific steps in the preparation of materials by which these aims might be achieved. We also emphasized, in a previous chapter, the need of setting down specific goals for each grade. However, in order to insure efficient and economic procedures in our progress, it is necessary to devise standards of evaluation, by which the achievement of our pupils in the various aspects of language learning may be measured objectively, in terms of the respective levels or grades and in the light of the aims which we have adopted.

A testing program is, certainly, not a mere incidental

step in the teaching process; it is an integral part of the curriculum in Hebrew. It should serve several purposes, administrative and supervisory, as well as instructional. It should help to determine promotions and to grade pupils, as well as subject-matter. It should also be utilized in evaluating the quality of instruction and the efficiency of the teacher, methods and materials. Above all, it should serve to diagnose weak spots, to disclose pupils' individual needs and abilities, and to aid in adapting methods and materials to meet these needs and abilities.

One of the least disputed principles in education is that knowledge of the extent of progress facilitates learning. Hence, frequent evaluation of learning-results, by means of a testing program, which demonstrates objectively, in a detailed and specific manner, the rate of pupils' progress, should prove helpful to the teacher and to the pupils, and should render the learning process more effective.

Objectivity in Testing

There are various aspects of language power which are essential in the learning of a new language, and for which the curriculum in the elementary grades, based on reading objectives, must provide. These aspects include the following abilities: (a) to recognize the meaning of a word in a sentence, (b) to translate an isolated word in the new language into the native language and vice versa, and (c) to synthesize in the new language, that is, to fuse and build spontaneously linguistic elements into a thought-pattern or unit, with the result of reading, with comprehension, sentences and paragraphs. The projected tests must be calculated to measure all these abilities *objectively*. Teachers' opinions and impressions are unreliable and are, furthermore, open to criticism. Classroom exercises, as well as the traditional type of tests, consisting of translations from and into the language or free sentence-building and composition have proved equally untrustworthy. Various investigations have demonstrated the existence of wide disagreement and differences in the scheme of marking, even among trained and highly objective graders of test papers. Even in such a supposedly objective study as mathematics, the range of difference in marking the same paper was found to be as wide as fifty per cent. Obviously, in the light of these facts the traditional subjective type of examination must be discounted as an instrument in measuring achievement.

The newer objective examination types, on the other hand, may be so constructed as to leave no room for suspicion of any bias or favoritism on the part of the teacher. They are easy to administer; they can be scored mechanically; and they lend themselves to simple and ready interpretation. These tests may also be administered and scored by outsiders, employing a uniform technique and procedure. This will remove any possibility of influencing the results by such subjective elements as variations in manner, procedure and general personality of the teachers. Obviously, this would apply only to the annual or semi-annual examinations, given on a city-wide basis. It would, of course, not be practicable to have outsiders administer the regular classroom tests which the teacher has to administer as need arises.

In order to insure further the reliability of the tests as accurate standards for the specific abilities, which are purported to be tested, it is advisable to administer more than one equivalent form of a test on the same level or within the same scope. If the scores yielded by two or more equivalent forms of the test given at successive days are approximately identical it is safe to regard the test as a reliable measure of instruction.

Some Guiding Principles in the Construction of Objective Tests

The objective type of test is gradually coming into its own as an essential tool in classroom procedure. But the construction of these tests is not as easy and simple as it appears on the surface. A number of requisites must be borne in mind and met before considering such tests satisfactory. These requisites are as follows:

1. The items selected for testing must be such as are regarded most significant in terms of the specific objectives of the course. This applies to vocabularies, grammatical forms, idiomatic expressions, etc.

2. The abilities tested for must, likewise, be such as are regarded most important in the light of the selected objectives.

3. It is advisable, in testing several specific abilities, to group the items in accordance with their particular category. Thus, one group may include items measuring ability to translate words in isolation, another group of items will test recognition of words in context, while a third group will call for comprehension of sentences or paragraphs. In this manner the test may serve effectively diagnostic purposes.

4. Avoid irrelevant material or subject-matter. In testing for knowledge of vocabulary do not include items calling for information involving a knowledge of other subjects, such as history or religion.

5. Keep the optional responses in the multiple-choice type of questions as consistent and homogeneous as possible in degree of difficulty, in grammatical category, in size, etc. It should be remembered that elimination of incorrect responses is perhaps as important a factor as the selection of the correct response. Hence care must be taken to avoid offering any clues which might

help the selection of the correct responses merely by easy recognition of the incorrect ones. Such clues might be the inclusion, in the optional items, of words which are either too easy or totally unfamiliar, a series of nouns plus one verbal form or vice versa, a series of single words plus one phrase or vice versa.

6. Avoid using sentences or contexts which are too familiar to the pupils because of frequent recurrence in the textbooks studied.

7. Do not employ in the optional responses words and phrases which are similar to those used in the question or in the incomplete sentence.

8. In questions on a given text or paragraph, avoid giving away in the optional responses the correct response by phrasing it in the language of the given text.

9. Arrange the items so that the correct response does not follow the order of any definite pattern.

10. When the object is testing for recognition of meaning, all extraneous activities, such as writing, should be reduced to a minimum. The mere checking of the correct answer should generally suffice.

11. The test should be comprehensive. It should comprise, whether in the optional items of the multiple choice type or in the elements specifically tested, all the vocabulary included in the wordlist for the particular grade, or a fairly representative sampling of it.

12. All words in the test, whether of the optional

or non-optional type, should be only such as are included in the wordlist for the particular year. This applies also to the English words in the tests, which are to be matched with the Hebrew. Only such English words should be included among the optional words, the Hebrew equivalents of which are within the framework of the pupils vocabulary.

13. Do not begin the test with questions that are too easy or too difficult. In the first place the pupils may get into an easy-going and lax state of mind, while in the latter case he may become discouraged and inhibited. The initial group of questions should be challenging but not overwhelming.

14. The directions for administering the tests as well as for the scoring should be simple and concise.

15. The test should be so designed as to allow the poorest pupil to get some score above zero and the best pupil to get close to the perfect score. An average of about fifty per cent correct is regarded as a valid criterion for a good test.

16. After administering and scoring the test it is advisable to go over the test-papers with the pupils in order to discover the specific and general difficulties encountered by them. In this manner defective and weak items may be uncovered and eliminated, and a more positive attitude on the part of the pupils toward tests may be cultivated. Children should, of course, be encouraged to comment freely.

Available Test Materials

Attempts at the preparation of objective tests in Hebrew with the view to standardization have been made recently by a number of communities. The Boston Bureau of Jewish Education is probably to be credited with having blazed the path in this field. For about two decades this Bureau has experimented with such tests and has administered them annually in the schools of Boston and vicinity. This Bureau claims to have made considerable progress in the direction of standardization.

More recently, Dr. Noah Nardi of the Jewish Education Committee of New York has been working assiduously on a series of tests on all the subjects of the Jewish curriculum, including Hebrew. The test for the first year in Hebrew is available in printed form, and is accompanied by a carefully constructed manual, presenting detailed directions for administering and scoring. It is based on the subject matter in Hebrew suggested by the Hebrew Principals Curriculum for the first year. This test has been statistically validated and includes two parallel forms, A and B.

The author, under the auspices of the Associated Talmud Torahs of Philadelphia, prepared a series of tests for the first three years. These tests are based not on any specific textbooks, as are the Boston and New York tests, but on the A.T.T. Wordlist comprising some 740 words, which had been compiled after extensive investigation (cf. Chapter IX). These words were distributed into three levels, corresponding roughly to the three grades or years of study of the Hebrew language in our schools, and tests for each of the vocabulary levels were constructed.

The types of exercises included in the A.T.T. tests are as follows: (1) Matching a word underlined in a given Hebrew sentence with one of four given English words, (2) underlining one of four given English words that corresponds in meaning to a given Hebrew word, (3) underlining one of four Hebrew words, which is the equivalent of a given English word, (4) completing sentences in Hebrew, in which a word is omitted and is to be supplied by one of four given Hebrew words, and (5) deleting extra words from given sentences, so that the sentences will make sense. (For examples see Appendix D). The tests for the second and third years include also story supplements accompanied by Hebrew questions on content. After reading the stories, the pupils are asked to answer the questions in English.

The New York primary tests contain features which neither the Boston nor the Philadelphia tests for the first year possess. They are: (1) Picture matching, that is, selecting one out of four words which match a given illustration; (2) paragraph comprehension, involving the choice of an appropriate answer to questions on the paragraph read; (3) grammar and writing, i.e., exercises designed to test the knowledge of certain simple grammatical rules recommended in the Hebrew Principals Curriculum for the first year, as well as the writing ability of the pupils. The real positive feature is the picture matching exercises, which are very good for young children. The paragraph activities are, in the writer's opinion, inadequate and inconclusive; while the value and need of the grammar knowledge and writing ability on the first year level are questionable.

The main weakness of both the Boston and the New York tests is the fact that they operate with a vocabulary which was selected intuitively. Thus, for example, out of about 100 words used in the New York tests for the first year, over 50 words are not included in the first year wordlist of the A.T.T. and rank very low in terms of Bible readiness.

Besides being based on an objectively selected wordlist rather than on specific textbooks, the A.T.T. tests possess other distinctive features worth mentioning. The relatively large variety of exercises helps to reduce the fatigue entailed by the monotony in the case of questions of the same type, and brings into play the various language skills employed in teaching, as well as in usage. These tests were designed to test for recognition of vocabularies in isolation and in context, as well as for sentence and paragraph comprehension. In all these exercises, however, the emphasis is on recognition and receptive knowledge, rather than on recall or reproductive knowledge, of vocabulary. Practically every word of the wordlist for a given year occurs at least once in the corresponding tests, whether in the items tested on, or in the multiple choice groups.

These tests have undergone several revisions with the view to improving their usefulness and reliability. Ambiguous and confusing elements have been, as far as possible, eliminated. Furthermore, dual forms of the tests are now available, which have been tried out on a fairly large number of pupils and have been found to yield approximately identical results.

The Problem of Standardization

An essential requisite for objectivity in testing is standardization, that is, the establishment of standards of achievement or norms. This can be done only under carefully controlled experimental conditions, where the number of variables is reduced to a minimum, which can be accounted for in computing the results. Specific instructions for giving the tests, scoring the answers and interpreting the results are to be complied with. The questions are then submitted to a large number of pupils, and on the basis of the average or the median in the results the norms may be established. These norms are standards of achievement, on the basis of which it is possible to compare pupil with pupil, class with class, teacher with teacher, school with school, and the like. They may also serve as a guide in the planning of courses, and in the preparation and choice of instructional materials.

Unfortunately, under the present circumstances in the Jewish schools, the teaching conditions vary so widely as to make the prospects of standardization of tests in Hebrew seem almost hopeless. Differences within parallel grades in intelligence and age levels, in hours of instruction, in teaching facilities, in methods and materials of instruction, and so on, render comparisons well-nigh impossible.

The most serious impediment in the way toward standardization is perhaps the variable of language material studied in the primary grades. The wide divergence of vocabulary in our elementary grade readers has been pointed out time and again. A test based on one series of readers will not do for parallel classes studying a different series of readers. The term primary Hebrew is meaningless as long as there is no general agreement on the common essential vocabulary to be included in such a course. Hence, the adoption of a wordlist, based on objective criteria, is an essential requisite for the standardization of tests.

The adoption of a common wordlist will, of course, not solve all the other standardization difficulties. Tests based on such a wordlist may not serve as an authentic yardstick by which to measure the efficiency of the teacher, the adequacy of the textbook, and the effectiveness of the method employed. They may, to a certain degree measure some, or perhaps all these items. But whatever they will or will not measure, it seems quite certain that we may then be in the position to establish definite levels of language mastery as goals which we should aspire to attain in the respective grades or years. Some teachers may attain these goals in the specified time; that is, the first level at the end of the first year, the second at the end of the second year, and so on. Others may be successful enough to achieve these goals in less time. Still others may be handicapped by local teaching conditions and may not be able to reach the respective goals in twice as long a period as prescribed. Pending more favorable conditions which facilitate the standardization of tests in our schools and the establishment of achievement norms, these levels of achievement will have to be regarded as theoretical and experimental, and comparisons will have to be viewed as inconclusive. Where teaching conditions can be approximately equated, differences in achievement as measured by these tests should be regarded as symptomatic of some deficiency and maladjustment that call for investigation and remedial measures.

Conclusion

The lack of standardization need not, however, detract from the significance of a testing program in our schools as an integral part of the general pattern of our curriculum. Such a program should serve as an index of direction and progress in our work. Regardless of what series of objectives we may adopt, there can be no question relative to the place of Hebrew as a potent medium for bringing our pupils into possession of genuine Jewish experiences throughout the ages. However, aimless and undirected teaching of our language in this country is bound to prove barren and wasteful. It may produce a great deal of motion without locomotion. We dare not trust to chance in teaching "general" Hebrew, in the hope that in the long run, our pupils will acquire anyhow the basic knowledge needed for appreciative and intelligent reading of our literature. In order to achieve our objectives in the teaching of Hebrew, we must, on the one hand, bring our methods of teaching into harmonious relationship with children's natural interests, and, on the other hand, equip our pupils with specific vocabularies, carefully selected and graded by objective criteria, with a view to unlocking the vast storehouses of Jewish experiences incorporated in our Hebrew literature. The acquisition of this vocabulary must be achieved in a reading context and setting, and tests should be designed to measure specifically this achievement.

To be sure, mere achievement in terms of skills, and abilities in Hebrew is inadequate. The concomitant attitudes, accompanying the teaching process, such as interest and desire to read Hebrew and to continue the study of its literature, are highly significant. Unfortunately, these concomitant attitudes cannot yet be measured directly and objectively by any available techniques. But we can and should measure step by step the extent to which we approach our goal quantitively and in terms of abilities. In the final analysis, success in achievement of abilities may serve as a fair, even if indirect, index of success in the development of concomitant attitudes. The two are intimately interrelated. The flush of successful achievement undoubtedly conditions the pupils favorably toward the subject matter and can hardly fail to foster an abiding interest in it.

QUESTIONS AND EXERCISES

1. What is the place of a testing program in the Hebrew curriculum? What are its purposes? How can it serve to improve the effectiveness of Hebrew instruction in our schools?

2. What are the advantages of the objective tests over the old-type tests? How can their reliability be established?

3. In the light of the criteria for objective tests given in this chapter evaluate some of the published tests available in Hebrew, such as those issued by the Bureau of Jewish Education in Boston, the Jewish Education Committee of New York, and the Associated Talmud Torahs of Philadelphia.

4. How can tests be standardized? What are the difficulties in the way of standardizing the tests in the Jewish schools? How can these difficulties be overcome?

5. Compare the words included in the above mentioned tests with the word list given in "Appendix B" of this volume. Criticize the choice of words in the tests for the particular grades in the light of the frequency and other values attached to them.

REFERENCES

COLE-THARP — *Modern Foreign Languages and Their Teaching*, Appleton, Chapter VII.

COLEMAN, A. — *Experiments and Studies in Modern Languages*, University of Chicago Press, 1934 (Tests in Modern Foreign Languages by V. A. C. Henmon), pp. 199–216.

GATES, A. I. — *Educational Psychology*, Macmillan, 1942, Chapter XVI.

FIFE, R. H. — *A Summary of Reports on Modern Foreign Languages*, pp. 98–129.

NARDI, N., "Manual for Interpreting Hebrew Achievement Test," *Jewish Education*, XV, 1.

APPENDIX A

Type Lesson Plan

(Note: The following lesson is a unit plan. A unit may take several sessions to cover. This lesson is presented in some detail for the benefit of the inexperienced teacher. It is, of course, to be remembered that the first steps in the teaching of Hebrew are presented here. Hence a good deal of English has to be used for purposes of motivating the study of Hebrew in general and of introducing the specific lessons. As the pupil's vocabulary increases and as his interest in Hebrew grows, a systematic effort should be made to reduce gradually the use of English and to create progressively a Hebraic atmosphere in the classroom.)

(Age Level: 8–9)

I. *Subject:* First Steps in the Teaching of Hebrew

II. *Text, Materials and Aids*

A. *Sippuri I*, chapters 1–4, pp. 1–9

B. Pictures of Palestine and of the objects and characters in the story.

C. Workbook to *Sippuri I*

D. Labels containing the Hebrew words and expressions to be learned.

III. Teacher's Aim

A. General

1. To motivate the study of Hebrew by dramatizing its use in Jewish life, especially in modern Palestine.

2. To make real to the pupils the environmental background of these stories in the Palestinian setting; and to identify them as keenly as possible with the characters and situations in the stories, thereby arousing in our children a vicarious need to learn Hebrew in order to be able to get along with the Hebrew speaking children of Palestine.

3. To develop in our children the ability and the attitude to approach Hebrew reading material as thought-content rather than as a mosaic of sounds and syllables.

B. Specific

1. To have the children learn to read with understanding the sentences and expressions comprising the following words: שם, ילד, ילדה, קָטָן, גדול, אב, זה, זאת; אַלָה, ילדים, ילדות, בית־הספר, בקר, הולך־הולכים, אֶל; גם, חכם, טוב, עברי־עברית, קורא, כותב, אין, אומר; רואה, מי, מה, הוא, כל, אחד.

IV. *Pupils' Purpose*

    1. To examine the pictures of Palestine and to learn something about them.

    2. To hear stories about a trip to Palestine made by a little American boy and his father; about the difficulties this boy encountered there in understanding his Hebrew-speaking friends and relatives, and about his efforts to overcome these difficulties.

V. *Procedure*

A. *Motivation*

    1. Refer to the pictures of Palestine. Ask your pupils whether they have ever heard of Palestine. Did they ever hear the Hebrew name of this country? Why is it called by this name? Draw out whatever information the children have about Palestine and its relation to the Jews, and enrich their background with some additional interesting facts and details.

    2. "Would you like to take a trip to *Eretz Yisrael*? Do you think you could get along with the boys and girls who live there? Could you play with them? Speak to them? Why not? Would you like to learn enough Hebrew to play and speak with the children of *Eretz Yisrael*? You see,

without a knowledge of Hebrew we are really unable to know what our friends and fellow Jews living there think and how they feel about *Eretz Yisrael* and about the wonderful things that are happening there now. Well then, we shall take a trip there, in our imagination, of course, with a little boy from Philadelphia, and we shall see how well he got on there."

B. *Presentation-Part I*

"I am going to tell you about a little boy whose name was שלום, who went with his father on a trip to *Eretz Yisrael*. For a long time his father had been promising to take him to *Eretz Yisrael*, the land about which he has heard so much, and about which his cousin שמואל, who had left for *Eretz Yisrael* about two years ago, kept on writing so many wonderful things.

One day in June, שלום and his father set sail for *Eretz Yisrael*. While on the boat, משה the father of שלום, tried to teach שלום some Hebrew, so that he might be able to converse with the children of *Eretz Yisrael* when he got there. You see, שלום was still pretty young and had not yet attended a Hebrew school. משה began by teaching שלום the Hebrew words for boy (ילד) and girl (ילדה). When they met a little boy or girl on the boat, משה pointed at them and said זה ילד (this is a boy) or, in the case of the girl, זאת

TYPE LESSON PLAN

ילדה (this is a girl). Soon שלום learned these words well enough to be able to use them correctly by himself. Whenever he saw a boy passing by he would refer to him by saying זה ילד, and when he met a girl he would say: זאת ילדה. From then on the words ילד and ילדה replaced entirely, in his conversation, the English words having the same meaning.

(NOTE: At this point the teacher should pause to have some incidental drill by having children refer to one another as זה ילד or זאת ילדה, as the case may be. Since the children are all beginners and probably unknown to one another, it will be advisable to take advantage of this opportunity and to use these sentences as means of introducing the children to one another in Hebrew. At this stage, the word שם should be added as, for example, שם ילד זה ..., שם ילדה זאת ...)

The next day משה taught שלום the Hebrew words קטן (little) and גדול (big); also the words אב (father), ילדים (boys) and ילדות (girls). And שלום was busy repeating these words on every occasion. He would keep on pointing at his אב, at the ילדים and at the ילדות, saying: זה אב, אלה ילדים, or אלה ילדות. He would also describe the difference in the sizes of the ילדים, calling one ילד גדול and another ילד קטן.

After learning all these Hebrew words שלום began to feel that he is quite a Hebrew scholar and that he would have no trouble holding his own in conversation with the ילדים in *Eretz Yisrael*. He will, of course, find out different later on, as we shall see. But before we go on with the story let us see whether *we* remember all these words which שלום learned so well.

C. *Assimilation Exercises and Application*

1. Have the sentences written on the blackboard and numbered. Read one of them and have the children, in turn, give the corresponding number of the sentence, read it, and tell its meaning. It may be advisable to distribute these three activities, so that all the children may be kept "on their toes."

2. Whisper one of the sentences, or have a pupil do it. Then have the children, in turn, guess the sentence whispered by watching closely the movement of the lips.

3. Have one child step out of the room, while another child selects one of the sentences. Let the child come back into the room and guess which sentence has been selected, saying: "Was it No. 4? (Reading it). And the class answers, "No, it was not" (or "Yes, it was") ... (Reading No. 4), etc.

4. Have pictures of the characters in the story posted on the bulletin board. Have the expressions describing these pictures placed on the chalk ledge of the black-

board. Call on some of the children, in turn, to attach the labels to the pictures to which they belong.

5. Read the lesson in the text. Have children number the lines, proceed as in number 1.

D. *Assignment*

1. Have children draw pictures of the characters in the story and label them appropriately.

2. Refer to the corresponding lesson in the workbook.

E. *Presentation-Part II*

1. Review. When שלום went to bed the first night on the boat he could not fall asleep. He kept on repeating the Hebrew words that he learned. And even after he did fall asleep he kept on mumbling the words in his sleep. Let us see whether we can recall all the words that שלום was mumbling. (Review briefly the words and expressions learned thus far by enacting the scene of שלום talking in his sleep.)

2. Well, שלום thought he knew a lot of Hebrew, didn't he? But he was soon to find out that you have to know a lot more before you can get along even in the simple everyday conversations.

The next morning, when שלום awoke, he was greeted by his father with the words בקר טוב.

"*What* is that," asked שלום, "I never heard these words before."

"That means 'Good Morning'," replied משה, "בקר is 'morning' and טוב is 'good'. When I want to say that you are a good boy I will say in Hebrew: שלום ילד טוב."

"And I guess," said שלום, "I would say: משה אב טוב about you."

"Very good! You certainly are a ילד חכם. You are not only a ילד טוב but also a ילד חכם, because you learn your Hebrew so quickly."

שלום guessed that חכם means "smart," and he was very much delighted with his progress. He could now talk about all his friend and about the ילדים he met on the boat, and call this one a ילד קטן, and that one a ילד גדול, this one a ילד טוב, and that one a ילד חכם. He also learned the word גם (also), and so he could go on recalling the names of all his friends and acquaintances and tell his אב what he thought of them. For example: יוסף ילד טוב, גם שמואל ילד טוב. אברהם ילד חכם, גם דוד ילד חכם. Then he thought of some of his friends whom he didn't like very much, and he asked his אב to tell him the Hebrew word for "isn't" (אין), and then he could say, for example, אין אברהם ילד טוב or אין שמואל ילד חכם, and so on. (NOTE: Have a little incidental drill on these expressions using classroom situations and experiences as illustrations).

שלום felt quite thrilled by his progress in Hebrew, and he was eager to learn some more Hebrew words.

TYPE LESSON PLAN

His father promised to give him another Hebrew lesson after breakfast.

When they finished eating breakfast שלום and משה sat down on the deck, in a corner of the boat, watching the waves.

"Now," said שלום, "let us have our Hebrew lesson, as you promised."

"טוב," said משה, "since we learn lessons here, we'll call this place בית הספר."

"I get it," said שלום, "You mean 'the school'."

"That's right," replied משה, "You certainly are a ילד חכם."

Then משה went on to tell שלום about the beautiful בית־ספר they will see in Jerusalem, where his cousin שמואל and all the ילדים go every בקר to learn עברית (Hebrew). There they learn everything in עברית and they speak only עברית. Even when they have fights and arguments they use עברית. Every ילד עברי in *Eretz Yisrael* goes to the בית־ספר עברי. Even some Arabic and other non-Jewish ילדים go to the בית־ספר עברי because the בית־ספר עברי is the best in *Eretz Yisrael*. Every one of these ילדים is קורא עברית and כותב עברית.

שלום listened attentively to all that his אב told him about *Eretz Yisrael* and about the בית־ספר עברי, and he asked his אב when he will begin קורא עברית and כותב עברית.

"When we come to *Eretz Yisrael*," replied משה,

"You'll go together with your cousin שמואל to the בית ספר עברי, and there you'll be קורא עברית and כותב עברית."

F. *Assimilation Practice*

(Follow the same procedure as in C).

G. *Assignment*

(See above D).

H. *Presentation-Part III*

When שלום and his אב, משה, arrived in *Eretz Yisrael*, they were met at the boat by the uncle and cousin of שלום, and they surely were given a warm welcome. The ילדים were very happy to see each other again. שמואל had already learned to speak עברית well, and he had almost forgotten most of his English, because the ילדים in *Eretz Yisrael* speak only עברית.

When the party arrived in Jerusalem, where the uncle of שלום lived, שמואל took שלום outside to meet some of his friends and to play. But שלום at first felt uncomfortable and unhappy, because he heard all the ילדים chattering away in עברית and he could not follow them, despite all the עברית that he learned from his אב during the trip. But gradually he began to regain his confidence and, as he listened very carefully, he found that he could make out a good deal of what the ילדים were saying.

He heard one ילד and then another ילד come over and point at him, asking "מה שם ילד זה? מי הוא ילד

זה?," and then heard שמואל answer, "שם ילד זה שלום," זה ילד מאמריקה," שלום understood that they wanted to know who he was, where he came from, and what his name was.

You see, if I wanted to know the name (שם) of this ילד (pointing to one of the boys), I should ask one of his friends whom I know: מה שם ילד זה? or מי הוא ילד זה?, and he would answer . . . שם ילד זה. (Stop and drill on these expressions for several minutes, having the children introduce one another by asking מה שם ילד זה? . . . etc.)

שלום was then very happy. He was all excited because he could understand the meaning of so many words in Hebrew. He recognized many of the words, and he interrupted the games or the conversation every once in a while to ask the meaning of the words he didn't understand. He found everybody very friendly and helpful. And whenever a new boy came over he asked שמואל: "מה שם ילד זה?", שמואל was very delighted to hear שלום speak עברית on the first day of his arrival, and he felt very proud of him.

When they came home שלום ran over to his אב all flushed, and he cried out, "אבא, I have only been one day in *Eretz Yisrael*, and I already know lots of עברית."

"Well, well," said משה smiling, "What do you know? Come, let's hear."

Up stood שלום proudly and said, "I know what the שם is of everybody in this house."

"Let's hear it," said משה.

"Well," said שלום pointing at משה: "שם אב זה משה," then pointing at himself: "שם ילד זה שלום," then pointing at שמואל: "שם ילד זה שמואל," and then walking over and pointing to מרים, the little sister of שמואל: "שם ילד זה מרים."

But just then everybody burst out laughing, and שלום looked around him with wide open eyes not knowing what it is all about, because he had forgotten that a girl is a ילדה and not a ילד. But then his אב reminded him that מרים is a ילדה and that he should have said: "שם ילדה זאת מרים."

שלום was somewhat disappointed at the mistake he had made, but he was glad to be reminded, and he promised never to forget the Hebrew word ילדה in referring to a girl.

I. *Assimilation Drill*

(Follow the procedure as above, C)

J. *Assignment*

(The same as above, D)

K. *General Review*

1. Suggest the idea of dramatizing the story up to this point. Encourage the pupils to participate actively in the selection of characters and episodes. Stimulate them to review the vocabulary in preparation for the dramatization. Plan several try-outs and seat rehearsals.

2. Have labels with names of principal characters (שם ילד זה . . .). Pin these labels on the characters on whom they belong. Have the pupils read each label as it is pinned on. As each character steps up and takes his place in front of the room, the children should be asked to read the labels.

   a. *Preparation for the trip*
      (1) Father tells שלום of the trip.
      (2) שלום packs his clothing.
      (3) שלום and his father bid the family good-bye and set sail.

   b. *Trip on the Boat*
      (1) משה gives שלום the first lesson in Hebrew.
      (2) The second lesson.
      (3) שלום studying and repeating the Hebrew words on his bed, then mumbling these words in his sleep.
      (4) The following day.

   c. *Arrival in Eretz Yisrael*
      (1) שמואל and his father meet the visitors at the boat.

   d. *Children go out to play*
      (1) Children gather around שלום and שמואל, asking: "מי הוא ילד זה? מה שם ילד זה?"

(2) שמואל answers each one in turn: "זה ילד מאמריקה, שם ילד זה שלום."

(3) שלום, bewildered at the beginning, later cheers up and asks שמואל to tell him the שם of all the ילדים. שמואל introduces them all by name.

e. *Return home*

(1) שלום tells his אב about his progress in Hebrew, and undertakes to introduce each member in the family by naming them in Hebrew.

(2) He points at each one in turn, introducing them.

(3) Everybody laughs when he designates מרים as a ילד. Father corrects him.

(4) שלום realizes his error, repeats the correct expression and decides not to repeat the error.

4. Review the labels

After the play tell the pupils that someone who can tell what the label says may take it off the character. Let the chosen pupils tell what it says. Let the whole class read it.

5. *Game 1*

Building up and tearing down

a. Have labels or cards with the sentences of the lessons covered and have children read them.

Cut up one of the cards or labels, letting the children say each word as you cut it off. Then place each word in the chalk ledge directly under the corresponding word in the label attached to the board, or in the line written on the board. Then let them say each word in turn as you remove it from the chalk ledge.

b. Build up the label again by placing each word directly under the same word on the board and letting the children read each word as you place it.

c. Tear the label down, or erase the line by picking each of the words in order and letting the pupils read it.

d. Let several of the pupils go through the same exercise and steps.

e. As soon as the pupils get the idea, divide them into two groups, naming one side גדול and the other side קטן, or similar designation, writing the names of the teams on the blackboard. Alternate in calling upon a pupil from each team to build up or tear down the labels, saying each word as he does so, keeping score of the exercise.

6. *Game 2*

Have a list of Hebrew expressions or sentences on the blackboard. Call on one of the children to come forward, stand up facing the class — his back to the blackboard. Have pupils give, in turn, the English translation of the sentences or expressions, which the child facing them is to translate back into Hebrew without looking at the board.

7. *Game 3*

Play Goose Pen. The teacher flashes cards to children in turn. The one who misses his card is a goose and he goes into the "pen" (some corner or place in the room). The "goose" stays in the "pen" until he "catches" someone by pronouncing a word correctly before the one called upon has time to answer. The latter then goes into the "pen."

Refer to Chapters VI, VII and VIII for further suggestions.

APPENDIX B

Functional Words and Expressions in the Classroom

איזה משחק?	היום יום ראשון
חַלק (חלקי) את הספרים (את הסדורים)	היום יום שני
	היום יום שלישי
פתח (פתחי) את הספר (הסדור)	היום יום רביעי
פתחו את הספרים (הסדורים)	היום יום חמשי
קרא (קראי) בספר (בסדור)	מחר יום ששי
קרא (קראי) בקול גדול	יום שבת.
מַהֵר! מהרי! מהרו!	בית הספר, מוֹרֶה, מוֹרָה
לאט, לאט!	שלום מורה
הרימו את הידים	שלום ילדים
אתה (הוא) קורא יפה	תלמיד – תלמידים
את (היא) קוראת יפה	ארון הבגדים
טוב! טוב מאד!	פשוט (פָּשְׁטִי) אֶת המעיל
עוד פעם	שים את המעיל בארון הבגדים
האם אתה מבין?	שֵׁב (שְׁבִי) על הכסא
האם את מבינה?	קום – קומי
כן, לא	שב (שבי, שבו) ישר
גש (גשי) הנה	הַס! הַסוּ!
סגור (סגרי) את הספר (הסדור)	מנוחה! בבקשה!
סגרו את הספרים (הסדורים)	הַקְשֵׁב, הקשיבי, הַקְשִׁיבוּ
אסוף (אספי) את הספרים (הסדורים)	היש לך ספר? עפרון? סדור?
מי חפץ (חפצה) לקרוא? לכתוב? לצאת?	קח (קחי) את הספר (הסדור)
	קחו את הספרים (את הסדורים)
	מי חפץ (חפצה) לשחק משחק?

251

APPENDIX A

אני חפץ (חפצה) לקרוא, לכתוב, לצאת
אני חפץ (חפצה) לשחק משחק
מי יודע (יודעת) לקרא?
אני יודע (יודעת) לקרא.
הנה ארון הספרים
שים (שימי) את הספרים בארון הספרים
תודה! סלח! סלחי!
פתח (פתחי) את המחברת
כתוב (כתבי) במחברת
אמור! – אמרי!
מה אתה (הוא) אומר?
מה אתה (הוא) שואל?
מה את (היא) אומרת?
מה את (היא) שואלת?
אני אומר (אומרת)
אני (שואל) שואלת
אני חפץ (חפצה) לשאול

שְׁאַל! שַׁאֲלִי!
שאלה – שאלות
תשובה – תשובות
השומע אתה? השומעת את?
כן, אני שומע (שומעת)
עפרון, לוח, חדר
קח (קחי) את העפרון
כתוב (כתבי) בעפרון
סגור (סגרי) את המחברת
הביטו אל הלוח, לך (לכי) אל הלוח
הנה הגיר, קח (קחי) את הגיר
כתוב (כתבי) בגיר על הלוח
פתח (פתחי) את הדלת (החלון)
סגור (סגרי) את הדלת (החלון)
זה שיר יפה, הבה נשירה
לבש (לבשי) את המעיל
לאן אתה הולך?
לאן את הולכת?
שלום מורה, שלום תלמידים.

APPENDIX C

Suggested Word List

NOTE OF EXPLANATION

The Roman numerals in the second column indicate the rate of frequency in the Bible, as follows: I:500–5,000 times, II:200–500 times, III:100–200 times, IV: 50–100 times, V: 25–50 times.

The Arabic numerals in the third and fourth columns indicate the frequency with which the words occur in the books of *Bereshit* and *Shemot*, respectively. There are very few, less than 200 words, occurring with a frequency above 10 in either *Bereshit* or *Shemot*. Hence, these were included in the figure "10+."

In the fifth column the order of occurrence in Rieger's lists is given. The numeral represents the order in terms of a hundred. Words in the first hundred words of Rieger, representing those of highest frequency, are designated by the numeral 1. Words in the second hundred — by numeral 2, and so on.

The checkmark ($\checkmark$) in the sixth column indicates the occurrence of the particular word in at least four of the seven textbooks examined.

The seventh column includes words which still function in our present Jewish environment: in the home, the synagogue, or the classroom.

Suggested Word List

א

שמושיות	ספרי הלמוד	רינר	שמות	בראשית	מקרא	
	✓	5	10+	10+	I	אָב
	✓	13				אַבָּא
	✓	4	10+	10+	II	אֶבֶן
		2	10+	10+	I	אָדָם
		4	9	10+	II	אֲדָמָה
	✓	1	7	10+	II	אָדוֹן
✓			10+	10+	I	אֲדוֹנָי
		4	2	10+	II	אָהַב
		4		1	V	אַהֲבָה
		4	10+	10+	II	אֹהֶל
		2	10+	6	II	אוֹ
		5	'1	10+	IV	אוּלַי
	✓	4	1	6	II	אוֹר

APPENDIX C

		מקרא	בראשית	שמות	רינר	ספרי הלמוד	שמושיות
אוֹת	(sign)	IV	4	10+	13		
אָז		III	7	9	2	✓	
אָזֶן		III	3	6	6	✓	✓
אָח		I	10+	9	2	✓	
אֶחָד		I	10+	10+	1	✓	✓
אָחוֹת		I	5	3	7	✓	
אַחַר		III	10+	5	2		
אַחַר, אַחֲרֵי אַחֲרֵי־כֵן		I	10+	10+	2	✓	
אַחַת		I	4	14	2	✓	✓
אַיֵה		V	3	1	18	✓	✓
אֵיךְ		IV	2	1	4	✓	✓
אֵין		I	10+	10+	1	✓	✓
אִישׁ		I	10+	10+	1	✓	
אַךְ		III	10+	5	2	✓	

שמושיות	ספרי הלמוד	ריגר	שמות	בראשית	מקרא	
	✓	2	10+	10+	I	אָכַל
		6	5	10+	V	אֹכֶל
✓	✓	1	10+	10+	I	אֵל
	2	2	10+	10+	I	אל
		10	5	9	II	אל
✓	✓	2	9	10+	I	אלה
		4	10+	10+	I	אלהים
		3	10+	2	II	אָלֶף
	✓	1	10+	10+	I	אם
	✓	4	4	10+	II	אם
	✓	9				אִמָּא
✓	✓				V	אָמֵן
	✓	1	10+	10+	I	אָמַר
		5	2	6	III	אֱמֶת
		1	–	..		אָנוּ

APPENDIX C

שמושיות	ספרי הלמוד	רינר	שמות	בראשית	מקרא	
	✓	2	3	10+	III	אֲנַחְנוּ
✓	✓	1	10+	10+	I	אֲנִי
		3	10+	10+	II	אָנֹכִי
	✓	2	10+	10+	I	אֲנָשִׁים
		6	4	5	III	אָסַף
		4	10+	10+	II	אַף
	✓	1		1		אֵצֶל
✓	✓	3	10+	10+	II	אַרְבַּע-אַרְבָּעָה
		8	7	10+	III	אַרְבָּעִים
	✓					אֲרוּחָה אֲרוּחַת־הַבֹּקֶר
✓	✓	5	10+	1	II	אָרוֹן אֲרוֹן הַקֹּדֶשׁ
	✓	1	10+	10+	I	אֶרֶץ
✓	✓					אֶרֶץ יִשְׂרָאֵל
	✓	5	10+	4	I	אֵשׁ

	שמושיות	ספרי הלמוד	רינר	שמות	בראשית	מקרא	
		✓	2	10+	10+	II	אִשָּׁה
		✓	1	10+	10+	I	אֲשֶׁר
	✓	✓	1	10+	10+	I	אֶת (אוֹתוֹ)
			3	10+	10+	I	אֶת (אֹתִי)
	✓	✓	5		4	IV	אַתְּ
	✓	✓	1	10+	10+	I	אַתָּה
		✓	3	10+	10+	I	אַתֶּם
		✓	4	7	2	V	אתמול (תְּמוֹל)
	✓						אֶתְרוֹג

ב

		✓	1	10+	10+	I	בָּא
		✓	10	10+	10+	II	בֶּגֶד
			7	5	8	II	בְּהֵמָה
			12	4	9	IV	בּוֹר
	✓						בימה

APPENDIX C

	שמושיות	ספרי הלמוד	רינר	שמות	בראשית	מקרא	
		✓	1	10+	10+	I	בִּין
		✓	1	10+	10+	I	בַּיִת
	✓	✓					בֵּית־סֵפֶר
	✓	✓					בֵּית־כְּנֶסֶת
	✓	✓					בֵּית־תְפִלָה
		✓	4	1	10+	III	בָּכָה
			11	10+	10+	III	בְּכוֹר
		✓	1	10+	10+	I	בֵּן
			4	5	9	II	בָּנָה
			3	6	10+	V	בַּעֲבוּר
		✓	2	2	4	IV	בְּעַד
			3	10+	4	IV	בַּעַל
		✓	2	10+	10+	II	בקר
			16	9	10+	III	בָּקָר
		✓	1	5	4	II	בקש

259

שמושיות	ספרי הלמוד	רינר	שמות	בראשית	מקרא	
✓	✓					בַּר מִצְוָה
✓	✓	13		8	IV	בָּרָא
✓	✓		1	8		בָּרוּךְ
	✓	12	3	9	IV	בָּרַח
		3	5	10+	II	בֵּרַךְ
✓	✓	3	1	9	IV	בְּרָכָה
	✓	5	10+	10+	II	בָּשָׂר
	✓	5	10+	10+	II	בַּת
		5	10+	4	III	בתים

ג

	✓	1	10+	10+	II	גָּדוֹל
		9	2	10+	IV	גָּדַל
		13	5	10+	II	גּוֹי
	✓	1	10+	10+	I	גַּם
		14	1	25	IV	גָּמָל
	✓			10+	IV	גַּן

APPENDIX C

ד

שמושיות	ספרי הלמוד	רינר	שמות	בראשית	מקרא	
	✓	1	10+	10+	I	דָּבַר
	✓	1	10+	10+	I	דִּבֵּר
	✓	1	2	3	V	דָּג
✓		11				דֶּגֶל
		9	10+	7	III	דור
✓		6			V	דִּי
✓	✓	8		3	IV	דלת
			10+	10+	II	דָּם
	✓	1	10+	10+	I	דֶּרֶךְ

ה

	✓	2	10+	10+	I	הֵבִיא
✓		6			IV	הבין
	✓	5	3	3	II	הביט
✓						הַגָּדָה
		3	4	10+	II	הגיד

שמושיות	ספרי הלמוד	רינר	שמות	בראשית	מקרא	
✓	.	13			.	הדליק
✓	✓	1	10+	10+	I	הוּא
		2	4	1	IV	הוֹדִיעַ
		5	7	9	III	הוֹסִיף
	✓	3	10+	10+	II	הוֹצִיא
		7	1	10+	IV	הוֹרִיד
✓	✓	1	10+	10+	I	הִיא
	✓	1	10+	10+	I	הָיָה
		4	10+	10+	II	הִכָּה
		5	4	10+	I	הֲלֹא
✓	✓	1	10+	10+	I	הָלַךְ
		1	10+	10+	I	הֵם
✓	✓	7		6	V	הִנֵּה
✓	✓	1	10+	10+	I	הִנֵּה
✓	✓					הַס

APPENDIX C

שמושיות	ספרי הלמור	רינר	שמות	בראשית	מקרא	
		9	6	8	III	הֵסִיר
			10+	6	II	הֶעֱלָה
✓						הַפְטָרָה
		6	10+	5	II	הִצִיל
✓						הַקָפוֹת
		10	6	10	III	הֵקִים
	✓	2	10+	10+	I	הַר
	✓	2		2	III	הִרְבָּה
		4	10+	10+	III	הָרַג
✓		11	6	4	IV	הֵרִים
	✓	10	10	4	III	הִשְׁלִיךְ
		4	7	10+	I	הֵשִׁיב
			2	8	III	הִשְׁחִית
		11	4	10+	IV	הִשְׁקָה
			10+	10+	III	הִשְׁתַּחֲוָה
	✓	11		2	IV	הִתְפַּלֵל

HOW TO TEACH ELEMENTARY HEBREW

ז

שמושיות	ספרי הלמוד	רינר	שמות	בראשית	מקרא	
✓	✓	2	+10	+10	I	זֹאת
✓	✓	1	+10	+10	I	זֶה
	✓	5	+10	8	I	זָהָב
	✓	6	5	7	II	זָכַר
		17	3	+10	III	זָכָר
✓						זְמִירוֹת
✓		1				זְמַן
	✓	4	+10	+10	III	זָקֵן

ח

✓	✓	1				חָבֵר / חַבְרָה
	✓	4	10		IV	חַג
✓	✓	4	1	1	V	חֶדֶר
	✓	2	1		IV	חָדָשׁ
✓		1	+10	+10	II	חֹדֶשׁ

APPENDIX C

	מקרא	בראשית	שמות	ריגר	ספרי הלמוד	שמושיות
חוּץ	III	10+	10	5	✓	
חָזָן						✓
חָטָא	III	8	6	8		
חטא – חַטָאת	II	4	7			
חַי – חַיִּים	I	10+	10+	4		
חַיָה	III	25+	4	8	✓	
חָכָם	III	3	9	5	✓	
חָלָב	IV	1	8	3	✓	
חַלָה					✓	✓
חֲלוֹם	IV	25+		6	✓	
חַלוֹן	V	1		11	✓	✓
חָלַם	V	10+		11		
חֲמוֹר	IV	10+	10+	7		
חָמֵשׁ – חֲמִשָּׁה	II	10+	10+	3	✓	✓
חֲמִשָּׁה עָשָׂר				15		✓

265

שמושיות	ספרי הלמוד	ריגר	שמות	בראשית	מקרא	
√	√	10		2	II	חֲמִשִׁי
		8	10+	9	III	חֲמִשִׁים
	√	10	9	10+	IV	חֵן
√		9				חֲנֻכָּה
√	√	9		1	III	חָפֵץ
		9	10+	4	II	חֹק – חֻקָּה
		11	9	6	II	חֶרֶב
		2	10+	4	III	חָשַׁב
	√	9	3	5	IV	חֹשֶׁךְ

ט

√	√	1	10+	10+	I	טוֹב
		11	10+	6	III	טָהוֹר
√						טַלִּית
		5	4	10	IV	טֶרֶם

APPENDIX C

י

שמושיות	ספרי הלמוד	ריגר	שמות	בראשית	מקרא	
✓	✓	1	+10	+10	I	יָד
✓	✓	1	+10	+10	I	יָדַע
✓		4			V	יְהוּדִי
✓	✓	1	+10	+10	I	יוֹם
✓						יום טוב
✓						יום כִּפּוּר
	✓	9	1	10	III	יַיִן
	✓	2	+10	+10	II	יָכוֹל
✓	✓	2	+10	+10	IV	יֶלֶד
		2	7	+10	II	יָלַד
✓	✓	5		1	IV	יַלְדָה
		3	+10	+10	II	יָם
		1	+10	+10	I	יָמִים
		7	5	7	III	יָמִין

267

שמושיות	ספרי הלמוד	רינר	שמות	בראשית	מקרא	
✓	✓	2		9	V	יָפָה
	✓	1	10+	10+	I	יָצָא
			10+	10+	II	יָרֵא
	✓	2	10+	10+	II	יָרַד
	✓	14		1	V	יָרֵחַ
	✓	8	1	10+	II	יֵשׁ
	✓	1	10+	10+	I	יָשַׁב
	✓	8		2	V	יָשֵׁן
✓		3	10+	10+	I	יִשְׂרָאֵל

כ

	✓	3	10+	10+	I	כַּאֲשֶׁר
✓			10+	3	II	כָּבוֹד לכבוד שַׁבָּת
		3	10+	10+	I	כֹּה
✓			10+	7	I	כֹּהֵן

APPENDIX C

	ספרי הלמוד	ריגר	שמות	בראשית	מקרא	
✓	✓	15		5	V	כּוֹס
		4	3	3	III	כֹּח
	✓	11	1	5	V	כּוֹכָב
	✓	1	10+	10+	I	כִּי
	✓	1	10+	10+	I	כָּל
		8	8	15+	III	כַּלָה
		10	10+	9	II	כְּלִי
✓	✓	3		1		כַּמָה
	✓	4	3	2	III	כְּמוֹ
✓	✓	2	10+	10+	I	כֵּן
✓	✓	6	2	1	III	כִּסֵא
	✓	2	10+	10+	II	כֶּסֶף
		6	9	8	II	כַּף
✓						כָּשֵׁר
✓	✓	1	10+		II	כָּתַב

ל

שטושיות	ספרי הלמוד	רינר	שמות	בראשית	מקרא	
✓	✓	1	10+	10+	I	לִי, לְךָ
✓	✓	1	10+	10+	I	לֹא
✓	✓	17				לְאָן
		2	10+	10+	II	לב, לֵבָב
		2	10+	10+	III	לְבַד (מִלְבַד)
	✓	10	1	4	V	לָבָן
	✓	12	1	2	IV	לָבַשׁ
✓						ל"ג בָּעֹמֶר
✓	✓	15	10+		II	לוּחַ
✓						לוּלָב
	✓	4	10+	10+	II	לֶחֶם
	✓	3	10+	10+	II	לַיְלָה
		5	1	2	III	לָכֵן
	✓	3			IV	לָמַד

APPENDIX C

שמושיות	ספרי הלמוד	רינר	שמות	בראשית	מקרא	
			10	10+	II	לָמָה
		5	15	7	II	לְמַעַן
		15	6	2	III	לְעוֹלָם
		2	4	1	IV	לְפִי
	✓	1	10+	10+	I	לִפְנֵי
	✓	1	10+	10+	I	לָקַח
		5	7	10+	III	לִקְרַאת
✓						לְשָׁנָה טוֹבָה

מ

✓	✓	1	10+	10+	II	מְאֹד
✓						מְגִלָּה
		2	10+	10+	I	מֵאָה
		5	25+	7	II	מִדְבָּר
✓	✓	7	5	2	IV	מַדּוּעַ
✓	✓	1	10+	10+	I	מַה

שמושיות	ספרי הלמור	רינר	שמות	בראשית	מקרא	
✓	✓	4	4	10+	III	מִהַר, מָהַר
✓	✓					מוֹרָה מוֹרֶה
		8	1	7	III	מָוֶת
		18	10+	10+	II	מִזְבֵּחַ
✓	✓	4				מַחְבֶּרֶת
		4	10+	5	II	מַחֲנֶה
	✓	4	10+	1	IV	מָחָר
✓		1	10+	10+	I	מִי
	✓	2	10+	10+	I	מַיִם
		4	5	9	IV	מָכַר
	✓	1	4			מִכְתָּב
	✓	3	6	10+	II	מָלֵא
		4	10+	7	III	מלא
		5	6	10+	II	מַלְאָךְ

APPENDIX C

שמושיות	ספרי הלמוד	ריגר	שמות	בראשית	מקרא	
		8	25+	4	III	מְלָאכָה
✓		9				מִלָּה
		4	6	2	II	מִלְחָמָה
	✓	2	10+	10+	I	מֶלֶךְ
			1	10+	II	מָלַךְ
	✓	1	10+	10+	I	מִן
✓	✓	6		1		מְנוּחָה
✓	✓		10+		IV	מְנוֹרָה
		15	2	10+	II	מִנְחָה
		3	2	2	III	מִסְפָּר
	✓	5	2	10	IV	מְעַט
		3	25+	5	II	מַעֲשֶׂה
	✓	1	10+	10+	I	מָצָא
✓	✓	13	10+	1	IV	מַצָּה
✓			4	1	III	מִצְוָה

	ספרי הלמוד	ריגר	שמות	בראשית	מקרא	
	✓	1	10	10+	II	מָקוֹם
			2	10+	III	מַרְאָה
✓		10				מִשְׂחָק
✓						מָשִׁיחַ
		3	7	10+	II	מִשְׁפָּחָה
✓		2	10+	3	II	מִשְׁפָּט
	✓	2	10+	10+	I	מֵת
✓	✓	7	3	1	V	מָתַי

נ

	✓	1	10+	10+	I	נָא
		6	2	1	II	נָבִיא
		3	3	7	II	נֶגֶד
✓	✓	8	8	10+	III	נגש
	✓	10	3	8	III	נָהָר
		7	10+	8	III	נָטָה

APPENDIX C

שמושיות	ספרי הלמוד	ריגר	שמות	בראשית	מקרא	
		2	10	10+	III	נִמְצָא
		3	10	10+	III	נָסַע
	✓	3	4	20+	II	נַעַר
		18	1	9	III	נַעֲרָה
		5	7	3	III	נַעֲשָׂה
		4	5	12	II	נָפַל
		2	10+	10+	I	נֶפֶשׁ
✓	✓	11	10+		V	נֵר
			10+	10+	II	נראה
	✓	3	10+	10+	I	נָשָׂא
		6	5	10+	III	נִשְׁבַּע
		10	2	10	V	נָשַׁק
	✓	1	10+	10+	I	נָתַן

ס

שמושיות	ספרי הלמוד	רינר	שמות	בראשית	מקרא	
	✓	4	10+	3	II	סָבִיב
✓	✓	6	1	4	IV	סְנֶה
✓	✓					סִדּוּר
✓	✓	4				סֵדֶר
✓						סֻכָּה
✓						סֻכּוֹת
✓		7	1		V	סָלַח
✓	✓	9				סִפּוּר
✓	✓	3	4	8	IV	סָפַר
✓	✓	3	4	1	III	סֵפֶר

ע

		6	10+	10+	I	עָבַד
✓		2	10+	10+	II	עֶבֶד
✓		1	20+	2	III	עֲבוֹדָה

APPENDIX C

שמושיות	ספרי הלמוד	ריגר	שמות	בראשית	מקרא	
	✓	1	10+	10+	I	עָבַר
✓	✓				IV	עִבְרִי / עִבְרִית
	✓	1	10+	10+	I	עַד
✓	✓	1	10+	10+	I	עוֹד
	✓	2	10+	10+	II	עוֹלָם
		9	6	4	II	עָוֹן
		4	3	10	III	עָזַב
✓	✓	2	10+	10+	I	עַיִן
	✓	2	10+	10+	I	עִיר
✓	✓	1	10+	10+	I	עַל
		10	2	4		עַל־דְּבַר
		5				עַל־יַד
	✓	1	10+	10+	I	עָלָה
	✓	1	10+	10+	I	עִם

שמושיות	ספרי הלמוד	ריגר	שמות	בראשית	מקרא	
	✓ ·	1	10+	10+	I	עַם
	✓	2	10+	10+	I	עָמַד
	✓	2	8	10+	II	עָנָה
	✓	8	1		IV	עָנִי
		13	3	8	III	עָפָר
	✓	2	10+	10+	II	עֵץ
	✓	2	10+	10+	III	עֶרֶב
		13	5	7	IV	עֵשֶׂב
	✓	1	10+	10+	I	עָשָׂה
	✓	3	10+	10+	II	עֶשֶׂר – עֲשָׂרָה
		5	10+	10+	II	עֶשְׂרִים
		6	3	10	II	עֵת
	✓	2	10+	10+	I	עַתָּה

APPENDIX C 279

פ

שמושיות	ספרי הלמוד	רינר	שמות	בראשית	מקרא	
✓	✓	3		3	V	פֹה
✓	✓	4	10+	10+	II	פָּה
✓	✓					פורים
			10+	10+	III	פֶּן
		3	6	3	III	פָּנָה
	✓	2	10+	10+	I	פָּנִים
✓	✓					פֶּסַח
	✓	1	5	9	III	פַּעַם
	✓	9	1	8	III	פְּרִי – פֵּרוֹת
	✓	5	6		V	פְּרָחִים
✓	✓	4	2	7	III	פָּתַח
		8	10+	10	III	פָּתַח

צ

שמושיות	ספרי הלמוד	רינר	שמות	בראשית	מקרא	
		6	10+	10+	II	צֹאן
		10	5	4	II	צָבָא
		6			III	צֶדֶק
✓				3		צְדָקָה
		8	3	10	I	צַדִּיק
	✓	14	10+	10+	I	צָוָה
				6		צָחַק
		7	10+	3	IV	צָעַק
		14	5	3		צְעָקָה
	✓	11		2	IV	צִפֹּר

ק

✓						קדוש
✓		9	2		III	קָדוֹשׁ
		6	50+		I	קֹדֶשׁ

APPENDIX C

	שמושיות	ספרי הלמוד	ריגר	שמות	בראשית	מקרא	
קוֹל		°	I	10+	10+	2	✓	
קוּם		I	10+	10+	2	✓	✓
קָטֹן / קְטַנָּה		III	10+	2	2	✓	✓
קָנֶה		IV	10+	2	3		
קָרָא		I	10+	10+	1	✓	✓
קְרָב (בִּקְרָב)		II	7	10+	8		
קֶרֶן קַיָּמֶת					6		✓

ר

רָאָה		I	10+	10+	1	✓	✓
ראש		I	10+	10+	2	✓	✓
ראש הַשָּׁנָה							✓
ראשון		III	10+	10+	2	✓	✓
רַב – רַבִּי							✓
רַב	°	II	10+	9	3	✓	

	שמושיות	ספרי הלמוד	רינר	שמות	בראשית	מקרא	
	✓	✓	9	3	3	V	רביעי
		✓	3	10+	10+	II	רגל
			8	5	5	III	רָדַף
		✓	3	10+	10+	II	רוּחַ
		✓	11	10	5	IV	רָחַץ
			6	10+	8	II	רַע
	✓	✓	2	10+	10+	III	רֵעַ
		✓	8	4	10+	III	רָעָה (v.)
			8	1	20+	III	רָעֵב
		✓	4		9	II	רָץ
			2	7	10	III	רַק
			11	4	3	II	רָשָׁע

שׁ, שׂ

| | ✓ | ✓ | 2 | 6 | 10+ | III | שָׁאַל |
| | ✓ | ✓ | 3 | | | | שְׁאֵלָה |

APPENDIX C 283

	שמושיות	ספרי הלמוד	ריגר	שמות	בראשית	מקרא	
שָׁב		✓	2	10+	10+	I	
שָׁבוּעַ	✓	✓	3	2	2		
שָׁבוּעוֹת	✓						
שְׁבִיעִי	✓		18	15+	4	IV	
שֶׁבַע – שִׁבְעָה	✓	✓	3	10+	10+	I	
שבעים			16	6	8	IV	
שַׁבָּת	✓	✓	4	10+		III	
שָׂדֶה		✓	3	10+	10+	II	
שׁוֹפָר	✓						
שׂחק	✓	✓					
שיר – שִׁירָה	✓	✓	5	1	1	III	
שָׁכַב		✓	4	3	15	II	
שָׁכַח			6		2	III	
שֶׁל – שֶׁלִּי	✓	✓	1				
שָׁלוֹם	✓	✓	1	3	10+	II	

שמושיות	ספרי הלמוד	רינר	שמות	בראשית	מקרא	
	✓	1	10+	10+	I	שָׁלַח
✓	✓	9	10+		IV	שֻׁלְחָן
✓	✓	5	5	7	III	שְׁלִישִׁי
		2	18	1	IV	שלם
✓	✓	2	10+	10+	III	שָׁלֹשׁ – שְׁלֹשָׁה
		7	9	10+	II	שְׁלֹשִׁים
✓	✓	1	10+	10+	I	שׁם
✓	✓	1	10+	10+	I	שָׁם־שָׁמָה
✓	✓	3	10+	10+	I	שָׂם
✓	✓	5		1	II	שִׂמְחָה
	✓	3	10+	10+	II	שָׁמַיִם
	✓	6	4	10+	III	שמנה – שמנה
	✓	17	3	6	III	שמנים
✓	✓	1	10+	10+	I	שָׁמַע
	✓	4	10+	9	II	שָׁמַר

APPENDIX C

שמושיות	ספרי הלמוד	ריגר	שמות	בראשית	מקרא	
	✓	5	4	6	II	שֶׁמֶשׁ
✓						שַׁמָּשׁ
		15	4	6	III	שָׂנֵא
✓	✓	1	10+	10+	I	שָׁנָה
✓	✓	2	10+	10+	III	שני
✓	✓	2	10+	10+	III	שנים
✓	✓	5	10+	10+	II	שש – שִׁשָּׁה
✓	✓	8	4	1	II	שׁשׁי
		15		8	IV	ששים
	✓	7	15	8	III	שָׂפָה
			1	25+	IV	שִׁפְחָה
		3	8	5	III	שָׁפַט
	✓	6	3		IV	שַׂר
			3	25+	II	שֵׁר

שטויות	ספרי הלמוד	רינר	שמות	בראשית	מקרא	
	✓	5	10+	10+	I	שָׁתָה
✓	✓	6	10+	10+	III	שְׁתַיִם

ת

✓	✓	5			V	תּוֹדָה
	✓	3	10+	10+	II	תּוֹךְ
✓		3	7	1	II	תּוֹרָה
✓	✓	4	10+	10+	I	תַּחַת
✓		3				תַּלְמִיד
	✓	5	8		III	תָּמִיד
	✓	12			IV	תְּפִלָּה
✓		2				תְּשׁוּבָה
	✓	7	1	10+	IV	תֵּשַׁע – תִּשְׁעָה
		20		5	V	תשעים

APPENDIX D

Samples of Tests for the First Year

Directions to Pupils

Before beginning the examination, please write the following about yourself Your name?   . . . Your address? .

Your age?   Your Grade in Public School?
    YEARS   MONTHS

In Hebrew School? .   . Name of your Hebrew School?   . . . . .
Name of Teacher?   .

Group I

For each Hebrew word underscored, there are 4 English translations Only one of these translations is correct. Draw a line under that English word or phrase which has the same meaning as the underlined Hebrew word Look carefully at the examples.

tree, chair, light, flower　　　　　　　הַשֶׁמֶשׁ נוֹתֵן אוֹר.

(Here a line is drawn under the word "light", which is the only correct translation of אוֹר).

Examples: the sun, the sky, the　　　אֵצֶל הַבַּיִת עוֹמֵד אִישׁ.
house, the tree

(Here a line is drawn under the phrase "the house", which is the only correct translation of הַבַּיִת)

the sister, the father, the　　　　1　הָאָב יָצָא מִן הַבַּיִת לַעֲבוֹדָה.
  brother, the mother

knows, prays, learns, goes　　　　2　הָאָחוֹת לוֹמֶדֶת עִבְרִית.

288 HOW TO TEACH ELEMENTARY HEBREW

3 הַמוֹרָה מְסַפֶּרֶת סִפּוּרִים יָפִים.   songs, stories, schools, books

4 הָאֵם נוֹתֶנֶת לַיְלָדִים אֲרוּחַת־הַבֹּקֶר.   sings, puts on, speaks, gives

5 בָּעֶרֶב אֲנַחְנוּ אוֹכְלִים אֲרוּחַת־הָעֶרֶב.   I, we, you, they

Group II

For each Hebrew word, there are 4 English translations. Only one of these translations is correct. Put a line under the one English word that has the same meaning as the Hebrew word. Look carefully at the example

EXAMPLE: brother, child, father, <u>mother</u>.   אִמָּא

(Here a line is drawn under "mother" which is the only correct translation of אִמָּא)

1 אֲדוֹנִי!   Sir, father, mother, brother

2 הֵם   I, you, he, they

3 רֹאשׁ־הַשָּׁנָה   Passover, New Year, Palestine, synagogue

4 טוֹב   bad, little, good, big

5 כֵּן   also, yes, that, to

Group III

Each of the following sentences is supposed to make good sense, when completed. After each sentence there are four words. One of these words is needed to complete the sentence. Draw a line under this one word. Look at the example.

EXAMPLE: הָאִישׁ _____ בַּסֵּפֶר   הוֹלֵךְ, אוֹכֵל, <u>קוֹרֵא</u>, יוֹשֵׁב

(Here the word קוֹרֵא is the only word which makes sense with the rest of the sentence. A line is therefore drawn under קוֹרֵא).

APPENDIX D

1 בַּ____הַזֹּאת יֵשׁ מְעַט מַיִם.   כּוֹס, לֶחֶם, דֶּלֶת, סֻכָּה
2 אַבָּא הִדְלִיק____שֶׁל חֲנֻכָּה.   חַלּוֹת, נֵרוֹת, בְּרָכָה, דָּבָר
3 הוּא לוֹבֵשׁ____חָדָשׁ לִכְבוֹד פֶּסַח.   בֶּגֶד, דָּבָר, בַּיִת, לוּחַ
4 אִמָּא____עַל הַנֵּרוֹת שֶׁל שַׁבָּת.   עוֹשָׂה, עוֹנָה, מְסַפֶּרֶת, מְבָרֶכֶת
5 כַּמָּה אֲנָשִׁים יֵשׁ בָּ____הַזֹּאת?   פֶּסַח, שָׁנָה, אֶרֶץ, כִּסֵּא

Group IV

For each English word there are 4 Hebrew translations. Only one of these translations is correct. Put a line under the one correct Hebrew word that has the same meaning as the English word. Look at the example.

EXAMPLE: stands   יוֹשֵׁב, שׁוּאָל, עוֹמֵד, חָפֵץ

(Here a line is drawn under עוֹמֵד, which is the only correct translation of the word "stands").

you (feminine)   1 הוּא, הִיא, אַתְּ, אֲנִי
here   2 פֹּה, בָּא, אַיֵּה, יֵשׁ
five   3 אַרְבָּעָה, שְׁלֹשָׁה, אֶחָד, חֲמִשָּׁה
with   4 אֲשֶׁר, אֶל, עִם, אֵיךְ
ten   5 אַחַת, עֶשֶׂר, שְׁתַּיִם, שָׁלֹשׁ

Group V

In the following sentences there is an extra word. Draw a circle around the extra word and the rest of the sentence will make sense. Look carefully at the example

EXAMPLE: הַשֶּׁמֶשׁ יוֹצֵא (רֹאשׁ) בַּשָּׁמַיִם בַּבֹּקֶר

(Here the word ר א שׁ is encircled, because it makes no sense in the sentence).

HOW TO TEACH ELEMENTARY HEBREW

1 הָאִישׁ סָגַר אֶת הָיָה הַסֵּפֶר, כִּי לֹא חָפֵץ לִקְרוֹא עוֹד.
2 הַתַּלְמִיד כָּתַב אֶת הַתְּשׁוּבוֹת חֲמִאָה עַל כָּל הַשְּׁאֵלוֹת.
3 מִן הַבֹּקֶר עַד הָעֶרֶב חַלּוֹן עָבַד הָאִישׁ בְּגַן.
4 הַיֶּלֶד נִגַּשׁ אֶל הַמּוֹרָה קָדוֹשׁ וְנָתַן לָהּ אֶת הַפְּרָחִים.
5 הַשֶּׁמֶשׁ נוֹתֵן אוֹר אַתָּם בַּיּוֹם.

GROUP VI (Taken from New York Tests)

Each of the stories below is followed by two questions. To answer them read the story first and then decide what word or words answer the question or finish the sentence. Then put a check on the line before the right answer.

EXAMPLE:

שֵׁם הַיֶּלֶד יִצְחָק. יִצְחָק קוֹרֵא בַּסִּדּוּר.

א. מַה שֵּׁם הַיֶּלֶד?   ב. מָה עוֹשֶׂה יִצְחָק?

___ סִדּוּר   ___ כּוֹתֵב בַּסֵּפֶר
_✓_ יִצְחָק   ___ קוֹרֵא בַּסֵּפֶר
___ יֶלֶד   _✓_ קוֹרֵא בַּסִּדּוּר
___ שֵׁם   ___ כּוֹתֵב בְּעִפָּרוֹן

1. לַיֶּלֶד יֵשׁ סֵפֶר. הוּא קוֹרֵא בַּסֵּפֶר.

א. מַה יֵּשׁ לַיֶּלֶד?   ב. מָה עוֹשֶׂה הַיֶּלֶד בַּסֵּפֶר?

___ סֵפֶר   ___ כּוֹתֵב
___ מַחְבֶּרֶת   ___ שׁוֹמֵעַ
___ עִפָּרוֹן   ___ יוֹשֵׁב
___ מַחַק   ___ קוֹרֵא

INDEX OF AUTHORS AND SUBJECTS

Aims, in teaching Hebrew, see Hebrew;
in teaching reading, see Reading;
in teaching *Siddur*, see *Siddur*
Alexandrian Jewry, 8
Alliance Israelite, 27
American Canadian Committee on Modern Languages, 29
Analytical examination vs. analytical pronunciation in reading, 138 f
Aspects in language learning, 13, 220 f
Associated Talmud Torahs, word lists, 160 f,
tests, 226 f
Audience situation, 105 f
Auditory presentation in learning, 52 f

Bahlsen, L, 35
Barish, L., 20
Basic Language, 148 f, 151 ff., 158
Basic Hebrew, see Word lists
Ben Yehudah, Eliezer, 27 f.
Bible, vocabulary of, 154 f, 188 f.;
curricular significance of, 184 f;
difficulties in teaching, 186;
linguistic difficulties of, 187 f;
cycle approach in teaching, 189 f.;
proposed anthology of, 190 f;
specific suggestions for teaching, 195–203, also 118
Blackboard, use of, 106, 109–115, 117, 122
Boston Bureau of Jewish Education; tests, 226
Brooks, F. D, 87, 130, 147

Bulletin Board, use of, 122 ff
Burton, William, 68
Buswell, G T., 74, 87, 130, 147

Caiger, S. L., 205
Chomsky, William, 20, 35, 161, 168
Chubb, P, 183
Classroom directions and vocabulary, 251 f.
Cole, R. D –Tharp, J B, 35, 52, 130, 183, 234
Coleman, A, 234
Comenius, 22
Conditioned Response, 53 f, 79 f
Conjugations, study of, 174 f.
Counts, George S., 92
Cycle approach in teaching Bible, see Bible

Devices and Games, value and proper use of, 102–105;
in reading, 105–119,
in phonetic training, 143–146;
in the use of word lists, 162 f,
in *Siddur* reading, 213–217
Direct method, 24 f, 31 f, 37 f, 57–60
Dramatization, 64–67, 117 f
Drill, see Habit Formation
Dolch, E. W, 130, 147

Eisenberg, A, 128, 205
Eliot, Charles, 83
Epstein, Izhak, 28
Exhibits of classroom work, 124
Eye movement studies, see Reading

Fife, R. H., 58, 168, 234

Flashcards and labels, 108–112, 114–116
Freeland, George E , 66
Freeman, Frank N , 135
Frequency of occurrence, of words, 17, 149–159;
of grammatical forms, 174
Functional words, 3 f.; 17

Games and Devices, see Devices and Games
Gamoran, E , 21
Gates, A I., 53, 55, 87, 130, 147, 157, 167, 168, 234
Gestalt principle, 26
Gill, E , 134
Goitein, S D , 205
Gouin, F., 26, 35
Grading, of vocabulary, 17, 98;
of pupils, 98
Grammar, 169–183;
need of, 169 f ;
functional approach in, 170–173;
content and methodology of, in elementary grades, 173–179;
in advanced grades, 179–182;
inductive approach in, 175 ff.;
rational-historical approach in, 181 f.
Grammar-Translation Method, 22
Gray, W. S , 130
Grazovsky, Yehudah, 28
Greenberg, Simon, 218

Habit Formation and language learning, general principles of, 36–50;
economy, 37 ff ;
self-activity, 39 f ;
specific practice, 40 f.;
correct start, 41 ff.;
attentive practice, 43 f ;
integrated practice, 44 ff.;
individual practice, 46 ff.;
tempo in practice, 48 f ;
purposeful activity, 49 f.
Hamitlamed series, 48
Handschin, Ch H., 35, 130, 183
Harper, William R , 149 ff , 168
Ha-Shitah ha-tiv'it, see Ivrit be-Ivrit
Hebrew, its place in the Jewish curriculum, 6–10;
reason for present indifference toward, 10 f ,
content and method in, 13;
aims and objectives in, 13–16
Huey, E B , 87
Huse, H. R , 32, 35, 135, 168

Independent silent reading, see Reading
Individual method in Hebrew, see Hamitlamed series
Individual practice, see Habit Formation;
in phonetic training, 133 f
Inference in language learning, 77, 139
Integrated practice, see Habit formation
Interests of children, 17;
in reading, 92 f.
Ivrit be-Ivrit, history of, 27 f ;
procedure and technique of, 29 ff ;
evaluation and critique of, 29 f., 31 ff.

James, William, 80
Jespersen, Otto, 60
Jewish Education Committee tests, 226
Judd, C H , 130, 147
Judd, C. H. and Buswell, G T , 87, 130
Junior Hebrew Library, 18, 100, 125 f., 165;
see also Word lists

INDEX

Junior Sabbath Services, 210

Kaplan, L , 205
Kimhi, Joseph and David, 179 f.
Kittson, E G , 35
Klapper, P , 88, 130, 147
Krause, Carl A , 35

Language, its national significance, 2–6;
 its relation to thinking, 2 f , 4 ff ;
 a basic subject in the curriculum, 7;
 specific principles of learning, 51–67,
 as habit formation, see Habit Formation
Latin, its influence on language methodology, 22
Learning, defined, 39 f , 120
Lesson plans, see Type Lesson plans
Levine, Samuel H , 218
Library, see Junior Hebrew Library
Liebman, M , 218
Linguistic development, 36 f , 51, 60 f
Local Atmosphere (Realia), 62 ff
Locke, 22
Lukens, Herman, 53

Manuscript vs. script writing, 134 f.
Margolis, M. L , 5
McMurry, C A., 183
Mechanical reading, see *Siddur*
Meek, Lois, 92
Mental visualization, 25
Methodology, principles of, 16–19, 33 f
Methods in language, see Ivrit be-Ivrit, Direct Method, Natural Method, Psychological Method, Translation Method
Millner, A , 218
Modern Foreign Language Study, see American Canadian Committee on Modern Languages
Montaigne, 22
Morris, Nathan, 21
Morrison, Henry C , 35, 69
Motivation, in practice, 43 f ;
 in reading, 107 f ;
 in learning, particularly, of the lesson in Bible, 197–201;
 in *Siddur* reading, 210;
 in primary Hebrew, 237 f.
Multiple Association and Review, 56 f
Multiple Sense Appeal, 55 f

Nardi, Noah, 226, 234
National language, see Language
National Society for the Study of Education, Twenty-fourth Yearbook, 147
Natural Method, 24 f
Non-Hebraic curriculum, 9 f.
Nudelman, E A , 48

Objectives, see Aims
O'Brien, J A , 73, 88, 130, 147
Occurrence-frequency, see Frequency of occurrence
Ogden, C K., 152 f , 158
Oral drill, 106
Oral reading, see Reading

Palestine, see Local Atmosphere, also 235 ff
Parker, S C , 69, 88
Peterson, H A , 135
Phonetic training, 131–146,
 defined, 133;
 purpose of, 131–134;
 nature and analysis of, 135–140,
 steps in procedure of, 140–143;
 devices and games in, see Device and Games
Phonic Method, 75–77, 80

Piaget, J., 60, 81
Posters, 124
Prayerbook, see *Siddur*
Projects and activities, 49 f., 100, 124
Psychological Method, 25 f., 59
Purposeful activity, see Projects

Questions and Answers, 59 f., 99, 106 ff., 118 f., 127 f.

Rashi's commentary, its place in teaching Bible, 191
Rappaport, I. B., 64
Reading, defined, 41 f., 72, 77 f.;
a basic problem in education, 70,
in Jewish education, 71, 84 f.,
objectives of, in the primary grades, 72 f., 75, 95;
in the more advanced grades, 83, 95;
physiological basis of, 73–75;
proper approach and method in, 18 f., 78 f.;
stages in learning, 95 f., 140 f.;
proper attitudes and habits in, 101 f.;
situations and stimuli in, 120–128
oral, 96 f., 100;
silent, 18, 97, 107, 113, 118;
games and devices in, see Devices and Games
Reading materials, choice and vocabulary of, 89 ff.;
content and form of, 91–95, 97 f.;
use of, 98 ff., 105–119, 121–125;
levels of, 125 ff.
Reading Program, its nature and procedure, 97 ff.;
steps in, 159 f.
Reading varieties and types, 208 f.
Realia, see Local Atmosphere
Recognition of words in reading, 135 ff.

Rieger, Eliezer, 153 f.
Rosen, Ben, 160
Rubinstein, S., 64

Sandiford, P., 55
Sayce, A. H., 60
Scharfstein, Zevi, 21, 35, 130, 168, 183, 205
Schechter, Solomon, 8
Schluter, L., 32
Scrapbooks, 125
Script writing, see Manuscript writing
Sentence, as a unit of language, 60 ff., 81 f.;
need of emphasizing, 103.
Series system, see Psychological Method
Shreve, F., 183
Siddur reading, significance of, 72, 206;
nature and objectives of, 297 ff.,
course of study in, 210 f.,
procedure in, 212; games and devices, see Devices and Games
Sifriyah La-Noar, see Junior Hebrew Library
Silent reading, see Reading
Smith, Nila B., 130
Smith, William A., 74, 88, 130, 147
Social Atmosphere, 62
Spanish Jewry, 8 f.
Speaking knowledge, 13 ff., 51 ff., 59 f., 62 ff.
Specific training in language, 13 f., see also Habit Formation
Standardization of tests, see Testing Program
Stormzand, M. J., 69
Sussman, Samuel, 218
Syllabification, 137 f.
Synagogue services, see Junior Sabbath Services

Tennyson, Alfred, 6
Testing Program, its place in the curriculum, 219 f,
traditional types of tests, 221;
objective types of tests, 221 f.,
principles of constructing, 222-225;
available tests in Hebrew, 226-229;
problem of standardization, 229 ff,
need of, 231 ff.
Textbook, see Reading materials
Thorndike, E , 149
Traditional Jewish attitude toward Hebrew, 1
Translation Method, historical basis 22 ff.;
weakness of, 37 f , 40 f ,
use of, 57, 107
Type Lesson Plans, in primary Hebrew, 235–250,
in Bible, 195–203

Uhl, W L , 130

Verbalization in learning, 51 f.
Vocabulary, method of presenting, 57–60;
studies of, 148–167

West, Michael, 21, 35, 151, 152, 168
Witty, P. and Koppel, D , 130
Witty, P., 92
Word-counts, 149–159
Word lists, trend of, 148 f.;
in Hebrew, 149 ff ;
Associated Talmud Torahs, 160
Junior Hebrew Library, 164 ff ;
use of, 161 f
Words, as instruments of thinking and feeling, 2;
as cultural deposits, 3 ff.;
defined, 155;
determination of "easy" and "difficult", 156 f
Yellin, David, 28
Yoakam, G. A. and Simpson, R G., 69

THE UNITED SYNAGOGUE COMMISSION ON JEWISH EDUCATION

[A joint commission of The United Synagogue of America and The Rabbinical Assembly of America]

ABRAHAM E. MILLGRAM
Educational Director

MORRIS S. GOODBLATT
ALTER F. LANDESMAN
Co-Chairmen

MAX ARZT
IRA EISENSTEIN
HENRY R. GOLDBERG
SIMON GREENBERG

JACOB B. GROSSMAN
LOUIS L. KAPLAN
ARTHUR H. NEULANDER
SAMUEL SUSSMAN